THE ROAD TO
SEVEN FIGURES

YOUR GUIDE TO
HOME SERVICE SUCCESS

ERIC SPRAGUE

WITH KATIE HARRIS
FOREWORD BY MICHELLE BLEVINS

The Road to 7 Figures
© 2024 Eric Sprague

This book is dedicated to:

My late father, Harold M. Sprague. He was always my greatest cheerleader and he believed that I could be successful even when any indications of success were not evident. I wish he could be here to share in this experience.

and

Howard Partridge, my coach, mentor, and friend. Howard's impact on my life, in both business and my personal life, has been immeasurable. Without his guidance and example, I could never have been in the position to write this book.

CONTENTS

FOREWORD

The people you meet in life rarely know the impact they can have on others. If I had to guess, Eric has impacted *many* more lives than he can imagine— including my own, while I was a very new business owner. He is always there to offer sound advice, share a good laugh, or both.

Let me tell you a story that I hope will bring a smile to your face; although, it's always funnier in person, right? But I'll do my best. It was a beautiful, sunny November morning on Captiva Island in Florida when Eric, his business partner Larry, and I squeezed into a tiny video frame on my computer to record a podcast together. And I mean squeezed. Arm movement was not possible. To be honest, I hate doing podcasts at events, and my equipment was . . . well . . . amateur compared to others, particularly Blue Collar Nation (more to come from Eric on that). I was nervous as heck about doing a podcast there, but Eric and Larry were end-lessly gracious.

It didn't take long after hitting the record button for everything to go downhill, in the best possible way for a podcast. The entire 45 or so minutes we spent chatting on camera were filled with ridiculous gig-gles and hilarious stories about Eric and Larry's time owning a carpet cleaning-turned-restoration company. Eric was not shy about sharing the mistakes they made, and how they learned from them. Anytime the words snuck through the laughter, they were full of experience, wisdom, and honesty.

To this day, I reminisce on some of the stories that came up on that podcast and in other subsequent conversations I've had with Eric. For example, the value of training your team in ways beyond the normal job skills, expanding your business exponentially by leveraging your core business competencies, being a *solutions*-based owner and salesperson, and perhaps best of all—creating a company where people not only *enjoy* working but also want to share their experience with hardworking friends and encourage them to join the team. It's not uncommon in the trades for competing companies to offer crews a few more dollars an hour to lure them away from their current employer. Imagine building a team and a company where the pay wasn't everything your team valued because you weren't just giving them a way to pay rent—you were giving them a career and a bright future. Eric has done all these things, often several times over, and is hyper-focused on helping other entrepreneurs, especially those in the trades, do the exact same.

More recently, Eric sat and talked with me about struggles within my own business. It was a problem of promoting from within, and moving someone from a place where they excelled, into a position that just was not in their wheelhouse. Instead of judging or criticizing me, Eric asked great questions and showed immense empathy. His help did not end with just this conversation. He shared stories of being in the same boat as a young business owner, and encouraged me through the journey. Eric shared internal documents from his own company to help me establish benchmarks and review processes for my team. Not only did he bring value through listening and coaching but he also handed me real, proven, actionable tools I could immediately take into my business. I never *asked* for any of these things; it is just who Eric is.

What you'll read within this book serves as proof of his big heart and immense passion for helping other business owners succeed. Eric's wisdom comes from both big accomplishments and big mistakes. I know this from the many conversations I've had with him over the years, and I am happy to say they have always brought me real and invaluable information.

I can tell you for certain that I am not alone in being grateful to Eric for the wisdom and time that he's given me. In a world where so many coaches and mentors push hype, grit, and hustle, Eric turns buzz words into true action steps and resources that lead down a common path on which all entrepreneurs can relate.

Now, he is bringing it all to this book as he takes you through the business journey—the value of the owner, basic and most important business concepts, and building a winning team.

I'll leave you with a question Eric recently posed in an article he wrote that was printed in the magazine I publish:

Are you truly putting the effort in to plan, strategize,
and figure out what will make you the best and most successful
version of your company that you can create?

If the answer is at all unclear, or a solid no, then this is the book for you.

Michelle Blevins, Publisher, C&R Magazine

ENTREPRENEURSHIP
IS ABOUT YOU. IT'S THE
SUM OF YOUR HABITS,
YOUR RITUALS, YOUR
LIFE SYSTEMS, AND
YOUR MINDSET.

INTRODUCTION:
IT'S ALL ABOUT YOU

As a business owner, you have had what business author Michael Gerber calls an "entrepreneurial seizure." This is when you have had a moment when you decide to start a business without fully understanding what it really takes to be an entrepreneur. You underestimate how hard business ownership is. You underestimate how long it will take to be successful. You underestimate the grit and determination it will take to make it, and you underestimate the toll business ownership takes on your health, your mental state, and your relationships.

Entrepreneurship is about you. It's the sum of your habits, your rituals, your life systems, and your mindset. You are the master of your own destiny. You will succeed or fail based on how you run your life and your daily habits. It sounds like a lonely road, doesn't it? Well, it can be. Conversely, it is also amazing. There are potential riches beyond your wildest dreams and true freedom to do what you wish each and every day of your life if you just do the right things to make it to 7-figures per year. Like you, I am an entrepreneur. However, it did not happen for me until I was nearly forty years old. I had enough of working for "the man" and I was determined to strike out on my own. There is a saying that entrepreneurs will work 80 hours per week to avoid working 40 hours for someone else. I think there is so much truth in this saying. I know this has certainly been the case for me on my entrepreneurial journey. You see, some of us are just not cut out to work for others. We bristle at the thought of someone else telling us what to do. We are mavericks. We like to chart our own course. We pride ourselves on not having to answer to others. We want to win or lose on our own merit and hard work. We want to participate in the American dream. We want to do it our way.

There is a problem though. As entrepreneurs, we now have absolute freedom, and in that lies an issue. We have too much freedom and too little training in the skills and habits that any entrepreneur needs to succeed. My business partner, Larry, loves to bring attention to the scarcity of real entrepreneurship skills that are being taught in schools or by our parents. He is right. Most of us had parents who spent their lives within the safe confines of a job. Punching a clock. Working for others is a trade-off. We trade the illusion of security for having the company tell us when we need to arrive, what to do all day, and when we can go home. The workplace provides a structure that most people need.

This lack of formal or family training leaves the new entrepreneur with little guidance for what really needs to be done on a daily basis to be successful. We start our business and just kind of make it all up as we go along. We work our asses off on a daily basis grinding it out to become a success, but often the success portion of this equation seems elusive to many of us.

Habits. Rituals. Executive function. Mindset. Turnkey. Systems. KPI's. These are the concepts you will become very acquainted with in this book. These are the components that make up the successful business owner. These concepts, applied on a daily basis with purpose and intentionality will be the fabric used to weave the beautiful tapestry of your multi-million dollar business. Business is really a series of consistent actions and habits, which when applied on a daily basis, will provide a formula for success. Our problem, as mavericks, is we don't like to follow rules. We want freedom.

However, true freedom lies on the other side of our daily habits. We need to get in tune with this. We need to embrace the formula for building a 7-figure business, and we need to implement the formula each and every day.

Let's talk about habits. Social media is full of memes and gurus pontificating about hustle culture, working "25 hours a day," Mamba mentality, and all that jazz. Give me a break. Those are great concepts for getting views and likes on a social media post, but the stark reality is nobody can live like this for very long. I tried, and it culminated with a trip to the emergency room for me (more on this later). When creating a framework for our daily habits, we need to ensure it has the following 2 ingredients:

1. Consistency
2. Sustainability

We need to leave all the social media stuff behind and realize our business is a marathon, not a sprint. We are in this for the long haul and we need to act accordingly. If you were to run a marathon, do you think you could run the entire 26.2 miles at your 40-yard dash pace? Of course not. Nobody would think that is possible. Yet, small business owners seem to be trying to sprint a marathon all of the time. In my business coaching practice, which is geared to help small business owners reach $3 million and above, we talk about this concept frequently. In fact, whenever I get a new client (they only reach out to me for help when they are in sufficient pain or frustration), all of them are in some state of burnout. The entrepreneurial mindset is to grind, to pick ourselves by the bootstraps, to hustle. All of this is true, we need to hustle and grind, but not at the expense of getting burned out. Burnout gets us nowhere. It's counterproductive. We need to have a sustainable daily plan to insure our long-term success, and we can't be successful if we are burned out.

The world's most prominent leadership expert, Dr. John Maxwell, often states, "If you show me your daily agenda, I will tell you if you will be a success or not." Dr. Maxwell understands what a properly planned day looks like. You and I are about to go on a journey of creating properly planned days, weeks, months, and years which will provide you with a blueprint to follow which in turn will act as the architect of your life and your business. Because for us entrepreneurs, our lives and businesses bleed into each other all the time. It's not like we have a job and once we clock out we don't need to think about it again until tomorrow. Our business follows us everywhere we go and in everything we do. There is constant pressure to grow and make good decisions. Payroll is hanging over our heads every week. We don't have the luxury to turn off and tune out for long, so let's talk about managing our lives, not escaping them.

Everything hangs on you. You are, in many ways, the product of your business. As with all valuable things, the product requires care and protection. So let's talk about protecting the product, which is you. But first, let's tell a cautionary story of an entrepreneur who did not do these things and paid the price.

SECTION 1:
YOU

THE BOTTOM LINE IS, IF YOU OWN A BUSINESS, YOU PROBABLY HAVE AN UNHEALTHY AMOUNT OF FEAR IN YOUR LIFE, AND THAT FEAR IS CHRONIC.

CHAPTER 1:
YOUR MIND

In 2015, I was in the thick of it trying to build my business. For years, all I did was work hard to be successful. I worked around the clock (literally, as I was on call 24 hours a day). I had constant cash flow issues. I was having problems at home due to my perpetual absence. My team had swelled to more than 30 people. And I was feeling like the business was running me, not me running the business. I was stressed out, unhealthy, angry, and depressed all at the same time. This was not what I had envisioned my life to be like when I started my business. The only reason I started the business in the first place was to have freedom and financial abundance. All I had now was pain and suffering. Something had to give . . . and it did.

One day during this period, I was exceptionally stressed and agitated. Around midday, I decided I needed to get outside to clear my head and work off my angst. I left my desk without a word to anyone and went for a bike ride. Although my lifestyle was quite poor and I wouldn't say I was in particularly good health, I was quite fit. I vigorously rode my bicycle 100 miles per week year-round. As I rolled out of my driveway, I knew something was not right. I felt out of breath and tight, so I decided to get off the main road and ride to the paved trail to avoid traffic. Once on the trail, I was out of breath on a terrain that normally was just a warm-up. Then it happened. I stopped my bike and pulled over to the side of the path. It felt as if an elephant was stepping on my chest. My left jaw and arm went numb. I had a heart rate monitor on, so I looked down at my bike computer and my heart rate read 208 beats per minute. That was more than double the normal rate for the effort. I thought to myself, here we go, I am having a heart attack.

There was nobody else on the trail and I was freaking out. I was worried I would collapse and die right there on the spot. My survival instinct kicked in and I went into action. I knew if I could just make it to the main road, which was about a half mile away; if I could keel over, someone would likely come to my rescue. So I pedaled for my life to get to the road. My heart rate was still through the roof, but I just kept trying to breathe. Once on the road, I was still alive, so I decided that I could coast back to my house. I made it home and then called Larry, my business partner, and asked him to take me to the emergency room. At the emergency room, they whisked me past the huge line of people and straight into the ER. There they gave me baby aspirin and took my vitals. My blood pressure and heart rate were through the roof. Larry was right by my side the whole time and in a moment I will never forget, I told Larry that I couldn't die right now because my wife and kids needed me and our employees needed me, too. It was truly the scariest moment of my life.

After batteries of tests and many hours in the ER, they released me. Chronic stress was the diagnosis and I was told to go home and rest and learn to cope with my stress better. For weeks after this event, every nerve ending in my body felt as if it resided on the outside of my skin. I was exhausted, weak, and scared. As I lay in my bed, I committed to change not only how I was operating, but how the business operated, too. I could not go on like this, and to be frank, nor could anyone else who worked for us. It was time to figure it out, and that had to begin with me.

CREATING A SUSTAINABLE LIFE

Entrepreneurs live a tough life. We have the stress of consistently getting the phone to ring, employee issues, and cash flow problems. We worry about the market changing, competitors, and making payroll every Friday. We feel pulled between work and our family life, feeling spread thin and the ever-nagging sense we are failing in all areas of our life. This wears on us over time. Therefore, we need to make a plan to care for ourselves.

Statistics show business owners are 30 times more likely to have ADHD, 3 times more likely to suffer from addiction issues, 10 times more likely to suffer from bipolar disorder, and 2 times more likely to suffer from depression than the general population.[1] Entrepreneurs are interesting folks who are amazing at what they do, but often need help taking care of themselves.

I also needed to learn to take better care of my mental health. If I was going to be a financial success, I needed my mind and body to be in a good place. So, I began to read, listen to podcasts, and ponder what I could do to manage my stress more effectively and still kill it at work. The first thing I needed to figure out was what were the major stressors in my life and what I could do to lessen their impact on my mental health.

Managing Time and Energy

The first thing I identified to be a problem was many of the people in my company created stress in my day by scheduling my time without consulting me. They would book me for appointments without asking me if that conflicted with my calendar. They would overbook my day and run down my energy. They would call on me for last-minute "emergencies" to fix. All of this was wearing on me. Since childhood, I have always liked to run on a strict daily calendar that was pre-planned based on accomplishing my

---

1 Source: Freeman, M.A., Staudenmaier, P.J., Zisser, M.R. et al. The prevalence and co-occurrence of psychiatric conditions among entrepreneurs and their families. Small Bus Econ 53, 323–342 (2019).

goals. Now, as an entrepreneur, I was living in a constant reactive state. Nothing good comes from this. I realized that to take control of my life, I was going to have to get ruthless. Ruthless with my calendar, ruthless with the people booking my time for me, and ruthless with myself to not overbook my life. In doing so, I sat down and made a *Success Requires Ruthlessness* daily sheet that I still fill out each day (more about this work-sheet later in the book).

Now, I list my primary objective for the day and how long I antic-ipate reaching my primary objective will take. Once I have written down my primary objective, I make a list of all the activities I will NOT engage in that day, such as scrolling Instagram, watching television, etc. I find it necessary to remind myself to write down what I will not do, so I don't lose valuable time on low-value time wasters. Then I make a very short list of the items I need to accomplish that day. I share this with my team and let them know they cannot book my time unless they get permission well in advance. In doing this, my team also has had to become better at putting out fires in the business and not relying on me to always figure out how to fix the problem. By letting go of the need to micromanage every problem in my business, I was also able to help grow my team members to become self-sufficient and more capable of helping me work on the business more, while they work in the business.

Energy Management

It is one thing to attempt to manage our time, but that does not really tell the full story for many of us. I have found that it is much more important for me to properly manage my energy as opposed to time. I often have plenty of time, but not the energy to do any more. Everyone has different levels of energy. Some of us are like the Energizer bunny and can keep going and going. Others, like me, are not blessed with as much natural energy and need ample time to replenish energy stores to be effective. This is a harsh reality for those of us who have huge dreams and goals, yet lack Ironman levels of energy. For us mere mortals, we need to create a plan to maximize our output during the time we are energetic enough to get things done.

First, we need to guard the energy we have. We cannot fritter it away on drama and extraneous things that do not serve our goal of business success. We need to manage our days, weeks, and months using an overall plan to be successful. I realized early on, that if I worked too many hours per day, I was burned out by Wednesday and my work efficiency really took a nose dive.

I hatched a plan I called "Blast and Cruise" to manage my weeks better and not lose steam in the second half of the week. I would "blast" on Monday and Tuesday, often working 12+ hour days and really getting done the key things I needed to accomplish for the week. By Wednesday, I would find myself getting tired and less effective. So, on Wednesdays, I would "cruise" spending the morning working on low-level tasks that needed my attention, but did not take much bandwidth to finish. Then, I would leave work each Wednesday and reward myself for my hard work by taking a several-hour leisurely bike ride, which was good for my mind, my body, and my spirit. Once back on Thursday, I would "blast" again on Thursday and Friday.

Over the weekend, I would "cruise" again, spending time with family and friends. I got outdoors to get some fresh air and exercise. I still always do some work on the weekends but not so many hours and usually work on low bandwidth tasks. This Blast and Cruise method has worked wonders for my work output and also my mental health. It has been a game changer.

Managing Fear

Entrepreneurs love to act as if they are bulletproof and have no fear. The ethos of hard work, pulling yourself up by the bootstraps, moving forward in the face of adversity, and all the sayings about self-reliance are definitely true when speaking about small business owners. However, what is rarely mentioned is how scared many of us are in the face of all the hardships of business ownership. We are on our own, and boy do we know it! We feel like we can never show weakness because our team members, our clients, and our families rely on us to be the strong ones. We are the people who eat hard times for lunch! We are invincible, except that we are not. We are human beings with all the same fears and insecurities as everyone else. Sometimes, we are even more fearful than others and try to hide our insecurities by being "the successful business owner." The bottom line is, if you own a business, you probably have an unhealthy amount of fear in your life, and that fear is chronic.

I know I have always lived with lots of fear and self-doubt—first as an athlete in school, then as a student, and then as a business owner. Fear has a unique way of motivating many of us. I used it as my prime motivator for many decades. I loved it when I was told I wasn't good enough, strong enough, or smart enough. These slights, whether intentional or not, were the fuel for my fire. These were the motivation to keep going even when I was exhausted or at the end of a long project. I also feared not being able to provide for my employees and my own family. If they were trusting me to provide a paycheck so they could eat and shelter themselves, then how in the world would there be room for any fear in my life?

I needed to focus on taking care of the people in my life. I was the strong one. I was the ideas person. I needed to never show weakness. The problem was, this was eating me alive on the inside, and it was soul-crushing.

Dealing with fear is a weird thing. You feel weak and guilty about even feeling fearful, yet at the same time, you want to get those emotions off your chest and talk about them, but who do you tell? You don't want to tell your spouse or significant other, they are relying on you to be strong. You can't tell your employees, that would make them feel insecure. So who do you talk to? Well, there are many options. Hire a therapist, a life coach, a trustworthy business coach, or a peer group. It is not healthy to bottle these emotions up for too long. Eventually, the truth will come out, so it's better to be proactive. For me to best deal with my entrepreneurial fear was to find a coach who would listen to me without judgment and give me actionable advice to help me lessen my worry.

Executive Identity

The last topic we need to address about the business owner mindset is moving away from a worker identity to an executive identity. This is a huge mental leap for many of us, especially for those in the trades. Many of us started as technicians and still think as such. We never really dreamed of scaling a business when we started—all I wanted to do was be my own boss.

Most of us got good at our trade and realized we could make more money for ourselves if we struck out on our own as opposed to working for someone else. The issue is, we are now that "someone else." We are the owner, the proprietor, the CEO. As we grow our company, our role changes, and to be effective, our mindset has to change along with it.

As I see it, the biggest killer of dreams in the small business space is the owner's need for control and not letting go to be able to grow. You cannot micromanage your way to success. My business mentor, Howard Partridge, told me to "build the team, or give up the dream." Howard understood this from his own business struggles. For him to live his entrepreneurial dream, he needed to build a great team and a business structure to support that team. Otherwise, you just end up owning a hard, frustrating job.

This mindset jump is easier for some people than others. Let me compare and contrast myself and my business partner, Larry. I have always viewed our business as an asset. Nothing more or nothing less. I am tasked with creating the systems, training, and environment where our team could add value to our clients, and they in turn, happily pay us for our work. Larry, conversely, viewed our business as an extension of his being. Anything good or bad that happened in our business, Larry felt was a direct reflection of himself. Which one of us do you think had a harder time letting go of responsibilities to the employees? Larry. Which one of us got more upset if employees made mistakes? Larry. Which one of us felt a larger void in his life when we successfully sold the business? Larry.

You see, it is hard to scale a business where you are the central figure in everything within the business. The #1 reason that only 5 percent of businesses ever reach 7-figure revenues is the owner not learning to act like an executive. The owner has not made the leap from employee to executive, and all that starts within the mind.

How do you learn to overcome this? I have a few ideas for you. First, look at your friend group. Are you still hanging out at the bar with the same people you have always had a beer with? How many of your friends are entrepreneurs? Do you still spend most of your time with your high school crowd? If so, you may need to look closely at your friend group. Dr. John Maxwell wrote in his best-selling book, *The 21 Irrefutable Laws of Leadership*, about the Law of the Inner Circle. In it, Maxwell states, "Never forget a leader's potential is determined by those closest to him."

So who is in your inner circle? What is their yearly revenue, net worth, and number of employees? Are you the biggest fish in your small pond? If so, it's time to find a bigger pond where you are now the small fish. Surround yourself with people who are smarter than you, richer than you, happier than you, and have bigger companies than you. In doing this, you will begin to learn how to act like the executive that you are and not like an employee.

Time

At a very young age, I began to realize the importance of time. It dawned on me as a teenager how precious time was. Time is the only commodity we cannot replace. Therefore, it is the most valuable thing on earth. Ironically, most of us fritter away hours, days, weeks, months, and years of our lives on low-value activities. We go to the bar every night and drink with our friends, we surf Netflix or social media for hours every day. We are just good at wasting time, even though we have a very finite amount. As

I began my career in the trades, I saw how valuable time really is. How little actual production time was available each day. We all squander so much of this precious resource. I was determined to make time my number one priority, even as a field technician. I decided I needed a constant reminder of the value of time.

So, I made a bold move. To keep a constant reminder of the value of time, I bought a Rolex watch. Now would my $39 Timex tell time just as well as my new, shiny $10,000 Swiss time machine? Yes, it would. Would my Timex be a constant reminder every time I looked down at my wrist to value and use my time wisely? No, it would not. I invested in my mindset by buying the Rolex, and in doing so, I took my first step toward learning about executive function and true entrepreneurial thinking. You see, one of the main reasons so many business owners never create a million-dollar business is how they think about their own time as a resource.

Time Management

As I spoke of above, time is not valued highly enough. Business owners often do not understand the true value of their time and in not knowing tend to partake in all kinds of activities within their businesses that are better left to be delegated to lower-wage employees. You see, your main job as a business owner is to grow the business. You are the one needed to chart the course and guide the ship. You need to be the one who gets the phones ringing, the business systems built and implemented, and the team trained to do the work. If you are an owner-operator, your time is even more valuable. You are often the most time-crunched of all small business owners.

Let's talk about how we manage time. First and foremost, we need to plan each and every day. We need to use a time management tool for both our personal life and our business. Why both? Because as small business owners, our entire life can be eaten up by our businesses and we can look back years later and not even know where the time went. However, do you know what business owners never miss or blow off? Sales appointments! We never miss a meeting where we can possibly make some money. For that reason, I have made it a habit to make everything important in my life a sales appointment. Date night with my wife, kids' ballgame, gym workout, and any other life events—all get put in my planner and are placed with the same level of importance as a sales meeting. You'll never miss a sales appointment, but you are all too willing to miss going to the gym or making it home for dinner on time. Plan this out and keep the promises you made to your calendar.

RECAP AND ACTION ITEMS

In this chapter, I recount a critical moment in my entrepreneurial journey that nearly cost me my life due to the intense pressures of running my growing business. My relentless work ethic and lack of personal time led to a scary trip to the emergency room, serving as a wake-up call to the unsustainable nature of my lifestyle. This terrifying experience forced me to reconsider how I managed both my personal health and my business. I adopted new strategies to balance my responsibilities better, focusing on effective time management, prioritizing mental health, and reshaping my role within the company to ensure both my well-being and business success.

ACTION ITEMS:

- **Time and Boundary Management:** I learned the importance of controlling my schedule by setting firm boundaries around my availability. I started using a "Success Requires Ruthlessness" sheet daily to outline my top priorities and clearly state what I would avoid each day, like unnecessary meetings or distractions. This approach helped me focus on high-value activities and taught me to delegate or refuse others.

- **Energy Management ("Blast and Cruise" Method):** I adopted the "Blast and Cruise" method to maximize my productivity without sacrificing my health. This involved dedicating myself fully to work at the start of the week ("Blast") and then switching to lighter, less demanding tasks mid-week ("Cruise") to recover. This pattern kept my energy levels balanced and maintained my productivity throughout the week.

- **Managing Executive Identity and Fear:** I had to transition from thinking like a worker to thinking like an executive, focusing on strategic leadership rather than daily tasks. Additionally, confronting the fears and stress that come with entrepreneurship was crucial. I sought professional support from successful friends and coaches, which helped me manage these challenges without letting them overpower my life.

These strategies underscore the necessity of self-care, strategic planning, and ongoing personal development to achieve lasting success and fulfillment in the entrepreneurial world.

AS ENTREPRENEURS, WE GET PAID FOR ACCOMPLISHMENT. PERIOD. NO MATTER HOW MANY HOURS WE WORKED OR HOW HARD WE WORKED IS IRRELEVANT. WE ARE TASKED WITH PRODUCING RESULTS.

CHAPTER 2:
YOUR BODY

It was the winter of 2009 and dumping snow in Utah. I looked out the window of my living room and the huge snowflakes that Utah is famous for were coming down hard. My Saturday was shaping up to be an epic powder day on the slopes of Snowbasin Ski Resort. Unfortunately, my powder day never happened. As I pulled out my ski gear, I could not even begin to zip up the zipper on my ski pants. I quickly tried on my ski jacket and I couldn't zip that up, either! What was going on? When did I gain so much weight? I had never had this issue before, but since starting the business, things had changed. I was fat and out of shape. I would skip breakfast every day. Then I would fail to pack a healthy lunch and end up eating fast food in my truck driving from job to job. Then stress eating would kick in each night on the commute home. My go-to was MacDonald's every night around 10 p.m. I would order 3 hamburgers, a box of 10 chicken McNuggets, a large fry, and a Coke. Then, I would wash that down with a Snickers bar or a bag of M&M's. This was my new norm, and it was not good.

Prior to starting my business, I had been a lifelong athlete. I was a three-sport athlete in high school, and after high school, I got very involved in lifting weights, mountain biking, and skiing. Athletics were my passion and I had taken being trim and in good shape for granted . . . then I found entrepreneurship.

I was so stressed and overworked that I sought solace in food. It was my escape. It was my new drug. The more I worked, the more I ate. Then we started adding employees and the stress ratcheted up higher. I just kept eating. My blood pressure was too high, my weight was rising, my cholesterol was through the roof, and I just felt like shit. In retrospect, I think I was punishing myself for not being better at the business. I felt ashamed the business was not growing at the rate I expected. So, the more ashamed I felt, the more I ate.

Something had to give. I was killing myself and I knew it. It was like some sort of protracted suicide. I needed to get a grip on my emotions and treat my body better. For me, all things start with a goal. I needed something to shoot for to make me dial down the eating and up my level of exercise. So, just like I did for my business, I sat down and started to dream. What do I like to do? What am I willing to do every day to get in shape? Are there any events locally I can do? Do those events scare me enough to go all in?

I settled on a road cycling challenge which was run by my local chamber of commerce. This ride was known to be one of the hardest around. It would be 100 miles with a timed section up the dreaded Glendora Mountain Road, a 9-mile-long climb in the steep mountains of Southern California. This event was daunting, and it scared the daylights out of me. I wasn't sure I could ride 10 miles, let alone 100. Being heavy, the thought of climbing a steep mountain for 9 miles was petrifying.

So, I did what any person with a goal should do—I announced to the public on both social media and at the chamber of commerce that I was going to not only participate but complete the "century" ride at the Tour de Foothills. I was all in now, I had publicly declared my intention and I had no option but to make it happen.

Just like a business goal, I needed to plan out perfectly this crazy goal I just announced to everyone. I had no real idea what to do, so I needed to seek some outside help. I figured I could learn from people who rode bikes, so I asked a few of the guys in the chamber if I could ride with them on their Saturday morning group ride. They happily agreed, and I showed up for the first ride on a cool and rainy day with a bike I barely knew how to operate, without any of the requisite cold-weather clothing, and wearing a pair of cycling shoes so tight on my feet (because I had gained so much weight) that I could not wear socks. I was out of my element!

We rode 19 miles that morning. I spent the majority of the time in the back of the group trying to hold on for dear life. When it was over, I went home and went to bed at 1 p.m. and did not get up until the next day. I was cooked. This made me realize I needed more than riding buddies. I needed a coach. I needed someone to guide me and teach me the right and wrong ways about doing this or I was never going to finish this big ride that was 8 months away.

Enter Jay. Jay had been a semi-pro mountain biker with a strong road cycling background. He was in a business group in which I was a member and I had heard him talk about his former riding career in a speech that he had given. I worked up the courage to ask him for help. I sheepishly told him about what I had planned and asked for some pointers. To my utter surprise, Jay not only offered pointers, he said let's start riding together at 5 a.m. daily before work. I jumped at the chance. Jay was going to help me reach my goal, and no matter how much I hated the idea of exercising at 5 a.m., I was all in.

So, every morning for the next 8 months, I was out on the bike learning how to train, to go hard some days and easy on others, what to wear, what to eat, why I needed a heart rate monitor, and all the skills to become a real cyclist.

As I trained for this event, my business and my life started to turn around. I was more focused at work as I had to limit my working hours so I could get enough rest for my training. I was in a better mood and it showed to my family, my team, and my clients. Most importantly, I had a healthy outlet in my life for my stress instead of allowing it to become destructive. I had a sense of purpose beyond my business, and it made me happier.

Jay taught me the concept of cycling is suffering. You do not try to avoid suffering in cycling. You lean into it. The faster you go, the more you suffer. This was such a revelation to me in business. If I embraced that being an entrepreneur is hard, I would be more willing to embrace the suck just as I was out on the bike every cold, dark morning. This new cycling habit I had taken up served as a metaphor for both life and business.

Now, I am not proposing you start cycling or do some immense physical challenge. These are personal decisions. However, for a myriad of reasons I think it is crucial to work on your health and fitness. It will look different for all of us, but it is important for our mental health, physical health, and self-esteem. Also, make it hard! Don't let it be easy all the time. Push yourself. Fail. Try again. The more we do this, the better we will be at coping when our business throws big challenges at us. We need to do hard things so we can toughen ourselves up.

I don't think I need to convince you about the importance of being physically fit and healthy. I think the main concern all entrepreneurs have is "When in the world will I have the time to exercise, cook healthy meals, rest, and recover?" Well, that is a hard one for sure. I know I have struggled with this over the years, but it is a false narrative. We need to do this. We become better at work when we are healthy and rested. We produce more and have better results when we feel energetic.

It is a balancing act and sometimes it does not all go according to plan. When I started my health journey, I was working 12+ hours most days. I had to get up at 4:45 a.m. to fit my workout routine. Did I ever miss a workout?

Yes I did. Too many to count. If I was out until 2 a.m. on an emergency water damage call, I certainly did not get up to train at 4:45 a.m. I slept in because I needed the rest. What I did do, however, was try to miss as few workouts as possible, I tried to sleep when I could, and I made it a habit to not quit my diet plan just because I had a hard day. My progress was not linear. I would have stops and starts, missed workouts, and had crummy meals. What I did not have was the mentality to give up. The business got in the way a lot of the time, so I did what I could each day and tried to stay on course as much as possible. The compound effect of not giving up paid big dividends over time. Just don't quit if it's not perfect. Never let perfection get in the way of "good enough."

If you want to get your business to 7-figures, you need the vitality and energy to do so. It does not matter what you do for exercise, just make sure you do something. Take a walk every day, go for a swim, take a yoga class, ride a horse. Do something you enjoy and be sure to do it consistently. It will make you happier, healthier, and on the road to becoming wealthier.

CREATING A DAILY RHYTHM

Having structure to your day is essential to being successful. Running around with your hair on fire during the workday may be your normal state of affairs, but to build a 7-figure business, you will need time each day to work on yourself and your business. Save working in your business for the rest of the day. MAKE TIME FOR YOURSELF EVERY DAY.

How do you do that? What does that even look like? Why is this important? How can I have "me" time when I have so much to do?

Let's start with creating a daily routine. Note that I did not say a morning routine. It is almost comical to me how many morning routines there are on social media, in books, and on the internet. I am not sure I have ever seen an evening routine. Look, morning routines are great and you should have one. However, we need to focus on a 24-hour schedule that is consistent and sustainable.

We need to look at the entirety of your day, not just what you do when you wake up. I don't care so much about when you do something. I am more interested in you getting done the key elements that you need to do each day, regardless of what time they are completed. Some of us are not morning people, we are night owls. A rigorous morning routine is useless to a night owl. It likely only adds stress to the night owl, as they have the stress of having to wake up hours earlier than feels good to complete a set of daily self-care tasks. Don't worry about when you perform your self-care routine. The only thing that matters is whether or not you are doing it. So, that said, let's get into what a good daily routine looks like.

After my health scare, I decided I needed a very strict set of habits and a consistent schedule to live by so I wouldn't fall back into bad habits. I am not a morning person, so I needed to create a system where I could get up at a reasonable hour to make it to work on time, but I did not front-load my day with the routine at a time that is not preferred by me. I set up my schedule to perform the majority of my self-care-related activities in the evening. If you are a morning person, you will likely get up very early and perform the majority of your habits before work. It does not matter when, just get it done.

PRE-WORK ROUTINE

The hardest thing for me was to get up and get going. In the home services industry, it was always an early start time and that was a struggle. I needed to make sure I got up early enough to get a few key things done before I went to work.

The first thing I always do upon waking is hop in the shower to start my day. Getting moving is crucial to my success as I am not a morning person. Once I am fully showered and ready for the day, I will take time to:

Meditate:

I know, I can hear you groaning now. Meditate? What kind of hippy shit is this? I thought the same thing for most of my life. I figured meditation was the kind of thing sensitive types did to get in touch with their feelings. After my chronic stress diagnosis, I needed to find a way to reduce stress and clear my head. I was turned on to meditation by a cycling friend who is a very successful entrepreneur. He told me that it had been crucial in his reduction of stress while running all of his very large businesses. Coming from him, I decided to listen and it was game-changing for me. I first purchased an app that taught me how to meditate. Without having a system in place, I would never have known how to start or what to do.

With the guidance provided in the app, I was taught how to meditate at the beginner level and then it gamified the process so I could track my progress and keep myself on track. The effects of learning to meditate have been profound for me. I am a person who is a grinder and I never just stop and take a deep breath. I am fond of saying I only have two emotions: winning and anger. Neither of those states really leaves me the inclination to care for my mental state. Meditation has allowed me to realize I can be successful without being frustrated or angry all the time. I can calm my mind to think more clearly and strategically. A clear mind is so much more productive; so, by working on this aspect of my care routine, I became much easier to work with, more collaborative with my team members, and just a nicer, calmer version of myself. Even if you think meditation is not for you, give it a try. In just 10–20 minutes a day, it can lessen stress and help you think through problems and create solutions to your issues.

Visualize:

The next thing I do after meditating is visualization of my goals. This is, what I want to drive, my home, my business, my bank account, and anything else that is important to me. Too many people never allow themselves to dream big. They get caught up in the little stuff. As author Steven Covey stated, they are "lost in the thick of thin things." Don't do this to yourself.

Sit down and figure out what you want and create a mental image of what your dream life looks like and revisit that place daily. The more realistic you can make it in your mind's eye, the more chance you will have of achieving it. It's like the phenomenon of you seeing a car that you have never noticed before and deciding that you want to buy one. Then, everywhere you go, you see your new dream car driving down the road. Our minds have selective attention. When we focus on something, our mind sifts and sorts for us, drawing attention to those important things we desire. So, if we visualize our dream life every day, our mind will help us focus on getting it.

Review Goals:

I believe in goals. I believe in knowing where I want to go so I can make a plan to get there. I believe too few people have a concrete plan to get where they want to go with their business and their life, and due to this lack of goals, they let life take them where it will. I started getting serious about goal setting as a young child. During Little League, I wanted to be an All-Star; so, I devised a plan to take ground balls, practice batting, and increase my physical fitness to be the best player I could be. I became a starting All-Star player.

When I was in college, I wanted to go to graduate school on a full scholarship, so I devised a plan to reach that goal. I got a full academic scholarship to the school of my choice. Once I arrived in the workforce, I wanted to make more money and get a better position. I started writing down my goals every day on a simple 3x5 card. Every day while working, I would pull out my 3x5 card from my back pocket and give it a quick read. Every night before bed, I would take a new 3x5 card and write out those goals again. I 10X'd my income within 5 years and got the promotions I was dreaming about.

This act of constantly being in front of my goals has led me to reach them much easier. Goal review keeps me on task and does not allow me to coast or stray from my plan. So, each night I rewrite my goals on a 3x5 card, and each morning I read the card several times before going to work. If you only do one thing in your morning routine, review your goals before heading out the door. It's crucial.

Eating:

I used to be a person who skipped breakfast, ate lunch at 7-11 (Red Bull and Doritos), and took a fast food drive-through for dinner. I was "too busy" to take time to make food and prioritize my nutrition. Obviously, this is not sustainable or good for your health. I needed to change my ways. All the blood sugar swings, salt, and sugar were messing with my head and my body. No amount of riding my bike was going to override this terrible diet. I needed to make a plan to better my health and also not spend all day in the kitchen. I started looking at ways to systematize the eating process. This required me to make a menu and a shopping list. Plan all meals a week in advance and do food prep on Sunday and Wednesday nights after work. My goal was to simplify the process and to make sure I always had the proper food on hand so I would not stop at a fast food restaurant or convenience store to quell my hunger. If we are the product of our businesses, part of our job is to eat well and fuel our bodies for business performance. We have to view food as a central part of our overall performance plan for our job and plan and eat accordingly.

Having completed my morning routine, I am off to the office for the day, armed with my cooler full of good food and a gym bag ready for a workout later in the day—I am prepared to take on all the day has to offer. This morning routine has completely overhauled not only my work performance but my life. By being intentional about how I prepare for the day, I arrive at the office in a better state of mind, I know what I need to do, and I feel great because I have invested in myself prior to arriving at work.

END OF THE DAY ROUTINE

After work, most of us are pretty tired. We just want to go home, eat a comfort meal, and veg out in front of the TV with our loved ones. However, if we want to be high performers and build the 7-figure business of our dream we still have a few things to do before we shut down for the day.

Accomplishment vs Activity Check:

Too many of us mistake activity for accomplishment. We get the endorphin rush of checking off boxes and finishing our to-do list, but rarely take the time to make sure those activities add up to the accomplishments we desire. Therefore, I encourage you to take 10 minutes at the end of the work day and sit down to review your day. What was the goal for the day? Was the goal reached? Did you do everything you set out to do or did you get lost in low-value tasks to make yourself feel like you were really working hard? As entrepreneurs, we get paid for our accomplishments. Period. How many hours we worked or how hard we worked is irrelevant. We are tasked with producing results. So be sure to take time every day to make sure you are really doing what is most important and not what seems most urgent.

Next Day Goal Setting:

After reviewing your performance for the day, it is now time to set your goal for tomorrow. Too many business owners walk into the office each day with no plan for future success. They work in a reactive state, moving from one crisis to the next all day until they run out of time or energy. This is a major reason only 5 percent of all small businesses ever reach 7-figures. The owner is not working each day with the end in mind and they arrive at work ill-prepared for creating success. Therefore, it is good practice to plan the next day with one major goal for the day in mind.

As mentioned earlier, my Ruthless Sheet helps me stay on track. The purpose of my sheet is to keep me working on my highest priority. The ruthlessness part is where I list out all of the things I will not do the next day to ensure I am on track to reach my daily goal. For many of us, we get sidelined with time-wasting activities. We surf our phones on Facebook and Instagram. We watch hours of Netflix. We take long lunches. We waste time on non-essential activities as a way to distract ourselves from getting to work. So, the first thing I do when filling out my sheet is to write down all of the things I will NOT do the next day. By writing down what I will not do, I make sure I will leave myself the time to get done the one thing that really needs to get done to build my business. I also have a section where I need to write down why I am working on the main task. What will the outcome be if I achieve this goal? The sheet helps me stay crystal clear about what I need to do and why. I do this sheet at the end of every workday to prepare for the next day before I leave my office.

Exercise:

I strive to do some form of exercise after work each day. I know many of you are morning people and like to get your workouts in before going to the office. That is great. I encourage you to exercise when it is good for you. I prefer to clear my head and unwind after work. I set aside one hour a day for the gym, a bike ride, or even just walking in the park. I find I am a better husband and father if I do some exercise after work each day. Daily movement not only helps us be more fit but it also helps us reduce stress and manage fear. Being an entrepreneur is tough stuff. We need to take a short period of time each day for our health.

Family/Friends:

One of the things many of us neglect as we travel on our entrepreneurial journey is the people closest to us. I certainly have done this. I lost far too many friends because I neglected to maintain our relationships while I was building my business. As for my family, I missed parent-teacher conferences, recitals, sporting events, wedding anniversaries, birthday parties, and much more. I have very few regrets in my life, but being an absentee father and husband for many years pains me to this day. In my mind, I was doing it for them. I justified my absence by telling myself I was giving them a better life. Much of that is true. However, if I am totally honest with myself, I was also doing it for me and my ego. I needed to prove to everyone I could be a success, and in doing so, I neglected those most dear to me. If you are doing this, please stop. Take a little time every day for family and friends. The business will not succeed or fail if you carve out a little time for your loved ones. Zig Ziglar once said, "Success at work is no replacement for failure at home."

RECAP AND ACTION ITEMS

Back in the winter of 2009, I found myself facing a stark reality: my health had taken a nosedive due to my all-consuming entrepreneurial lifestyle. Once a dedicated athlete, I was shocked to discover that I could no longer fit into my ski gear. This moment of truth highlighted the severe impact of my daily habits, which had devolved into skipping meals and stress-eating fast food, resulting in dangerously high blood pressure and cholesterol.

Driven by a need for drastic change, I set a formidable goal that both scared and motivated me: to complete a demanding 100-mile cycling event. Recognizing the importance of accountability, I took the bold step of publicly declaring my goal. I announced my intentions to friends and family, and on social media, which committed me to the path ahead with no room for backtracking.

I sought the camaraderie and expertise of a local cycling group and the guidance of Jay, a semi-pro cyclist, who became my mentor. Under his tutelage, I embarked on a rigorous training regimen. This journey was about more than just regaining my fitness; it taught me valuable lessons about persistence, discipline, and balance that translated well beyond the cycling track and into my business and personal life.

For anyone looking to tackle their own challenges, here are three actionable steps based on my experience:

ACTION ITEMS:

- Set Ambitious Goals: Choose a goal that truly challenges you, ensuring it is specific, measurable, and bound by a clear timeline.

- Declare Your Intentions Publicly: Make your goals known to create a layer of accountability that compels you to push forward.

- Seek Support and Guidance: Surround yourself with mentors and peers who can provide the necessary support and advice as you pursue your goals.

Adopting these strategies not only helped me achieve my fitness goals but also brought significant improvements to my business and personal life. The journey taught me the importance of aligning my daily actions with my long-term aspirations.

TO SCALE A BUSINESS TO 7 FIGURES AND BEYOND, THE OWNER NEEDS TO ACQUIRE THE SKILLS TO BE VERY GOOD WITH PEOPLE BOTH INSIDE AND OUTSIDE OF THEIR ORGANIZATION.

CHAPTER 3:

LEARNING EXECUTIVE FUNCTION

Executive function is a term used in neuroscience and psychology to describe a set of cognitive processes that are necessary for the cognitive control of behavior. That's a fancy way of saying you need to learn a group of particular skills to be able to run and grow your small business. These are your CEO skills. The skills that pay the bills. Most of us are not born with all of them. However, we need to develop some of these skills as we grow into the leadership of our company.

There are academic and scientific "book" definitions of necessary skills. As someone who has been on this journey, I will go through the most crucial ones that need to be acquired as a small business owner. I'll share why they are important, and how to train yourself to be good at them.

IMPLEMENTATION

Many entrepreneurial dreams are dashed because the owner cannot implement them. You know the type of person who does this. They have elaborate dreams and ideas about every part of the business. How the vans will look, the cool logo, the slogans, the branding. They tell anyone who will listen how awesome the business will be. How customers will line up to use their new company. Then, nothing happens. No sales, no marketing, no cool van wraps, no branding, no nothing. It's because the owner failed to implement them.

Many business owners spend too much time daydreaming and not enough time implementing what needs to be done to grow a business. Good business owners are implementors by nature. They create a plan of action and then get to the hard work of doing all the things it takes to make the plan a reality. The power is in the doing, not the dreaming. If you are to ever build a business, you must become very good at implementing the tasks needed to grow the business. Maybe it's going out knocking on doors every day. Maybe it's hiring the right marketing company. Maybe you need to interview and hire the employee who will make your business thrive. You must do it, every day and all day. This is the main factor between success and failure for most entrepreneurs.

EMOTIONAL CONTROL

Have you ever worked for a boss who lacked emotional control? I bet you have. That might be why you decided to go work for yourself. In my career in the trades, I have endured some of the most insufferable people in the world. Managers who would yell at employees and clients alike. Managers who would degrade and demoralize their staff. These people had no control over their emotions. Nobody wants to deal with the person who is up and down. It feels unstable and unsafe. One minute the person is telling you how great you are, the next moment they are yelling at you. I even visited a company once where when I showed up, the owner was crying uncontrollably because things in the company were not to his liking. I asked one of his employees if he was going to be ok. The employee's response to me was "he is always crying, we have just learned to work around it." This is not how you build a great business. We need to exhibit emotional control at all times at work. This is the mark of a professional.

One of my favorite authors is Simon Sinek. Sinek often writes about the concept of stability in the workplace for team members. Sinek's premise is employees need to feel stable and trust their leaders and their colleagues. This trust fosters cooperation, which Sinek believes is essential for the success of any group or organization.

If our job is to lead our company, we need to be able to control ourselves. Some of the best ways to work on this is to become:

- **Become Self-Aware**: Use a tool like the ***DISC Human Model of Behavior*** to better understand yourself. A tool like DISC will help you understand why and how you behave as you do. The better we understand ourselves, the more control we will have when we encounter things that create emotional instability within us.

- **Reflect:** Have you ever flown off the handle in anger and wondered afterward why you got so mad? I sure have, and that's not a great feeling. When things are not going your way or you have behaved in a manner that you feel is not ideal, take time to reflect on what led to your behavior and create a plan to fix it.

- **Practice Delayed Response:** This has been a game changer in my personal and professional life. I have an Irish temper and I have been known to not keep my cool in the moment. When I was younger, if there was an issue I did not like, I would often blow my cool right then and there. I realized if I was going to build the type of company I desired, I would need to learn to change my approach. I learned to practice the art of delayed response. Now, when confronted with a negative or triggering situation, I have learned to "sleep on it" and wait until the next day to deal with the matter. I want to have a cooling-off period so I can engage an employee with the respect they deserve and meet with them about the issue, not how I felt about the issue in that moment. This is not always easy to do, but learn to delay your response. Take a walk, write the email and don't hit send until you read it the next day, set a meeting with a staffer for the next day. Give yourself the ability to respond once you have had some time to cool down and really think about what an appropriate response would be.

- **Plan and Prioritize:** Planning is a key element of business success. Taking the time to slow down and plan what needs to be done and who is going to do it is crucial to run a growing company. Your key role is to create a vision and then map out how to create your vision, what goals need to be met, who will do these tasks (delegation), and how to keep everyone on track and measure success.

  The issue is, very often the bandwidths of small business owners are tapped out and they go into survival mode in the business very early on. Instead of stepping back and planning to win, they live in a reactive state and just hang on for dear life for the remainder of the life cycle of the business. This is one of the reasons so few businesses fail to reach the per-year benchmark. The owner fails to set aside time (and energy) to properly plan and prioritize what needs to be done to reach the goals of the business.

- **Focus:** Many of us entrepreneurs self-report attention deficit and focus issues, myself included. We are often really good at wearing a lot of hats in our businesses. Wearing many hats in a business is a positive trait in start-up mode, but as the business matures, the owner will need to transition to more focused roles as the business grows and changes. This is where many businesses seem to stall out. The owner is used to running around like a firefighter, putting out fires in the business, while in reality they should be focused on building the systems needed and hiring and training the team they need to not have as many fires in the first place.

Many owners don't know what to do next, so instead of figuring out the skills that are required for them to grow, they fill their time with low-value tasks where they already excel. This gives them a false sense that they are winning at work. A lack of focus can come from many of the stresses we are constantly under, such as:

3. *Decision Fatigue*: Constant decision-making can be mentally exhausting. Over time, the quality of decisions can decline, leading to reduced focus and potentially poorer choices.

4. *Burnout*: Long hours, high stress, and the emotional roller coaster of starting and running a business can lead to burnout, which can manifest as decreased concentration and focus.

5. *Information Overload*: In today's digital age, entrepreneurs are bombarded with a plethora of information from various sources— be it emails, social media, news, or industry updates. Sifting through and processing this information can be overwhelming and distracting.

6. *Fear of Missing Out (FOMO)*: The desire to capitalize on every opportunity can lead entrepreneurs to overextend themselves, leading to scattered focus and a lack of depth in any one area.

7. *Lack of Delegation*: Some entrepreneurs struggle with delegation, feeling the need to oversee or be involved in every aspect of their business. This can spread their attention thin and reduce their ability to focus on key priorities.

PEOPLE SKILLS

Our last topic within the "executive function" conversation is the ability to read and understand people. Emotional intelligence is a very important trait to have to guide a team, create great vendor relations, and serve clients in a way they like to be treated. In the home services space, it is not uncommon to see an owner with a very low level of interpersonal understanding and empathy for others.

Many of us came up in the trade as technicians. We were tasked with doing jobs on budget, making sure the equipment worked, learning very technical skills to hone our craft. People skills were not even a point of discussion. I know for myself, I cannot remember one conversation when I was a technician about my interpersonal skills. My conversations with managers and owners were always about how fast I could do it and not get a callback.

It makes sense that many technicians who have struck out on their own may lack the requisite people skills needed to effectively lead a team. I cannot tell you how many companies I have visited where the owner ruled with an iron fist and was fond of barking orders at his employees. These companies rarely keep good talent in the building and often end up slowly reverting to an owner going back to being an owner/operator because he "can't find any good help."

To scale a business to 7-figures and beyond, the owner needs to acquire the skills to be very good with people both inside and outside of their organization. Those skills can be built up by:

- **Self-awareness:** Understand your strengths and weaknesses. This can be done through self-reflection, feedback from peers, or even personality assessments. Using a tool like DISC, as mentioned before, is a great way to better understand yourself and others.

- **Local Community Colleges or Universities**: Many educational institutions offer courses in leadership, management, communication, and other interpersonal skills areas.

- **Online Learning Platforms**:
  » *Coursera*: Offers courses from universities and colleges around the world on a wide variety of topics.

- » *Udemy*: Has a plethora of courses on soft skills, leadership, and management.

- » *LinkedIn Learning*: Provides a variety of professional courses, including interpersonal skills and leadership.

- **Coaching and Mentoring**: Hiring a personal coach or seeking out a mentor in your industry can provide tailored advice and training. This one-on-one approach can be beneficial for addressing specific challenges or goals.

- **Books and Audio Books**: Many renowned books delve into interpersonal skills, leadership, and management. Some classics include "How to Win Friends and Influence People" by Dale Carnegie, "Emotional Intelligence" by Daniel Goleman, and "The Five Dysfunctions of a Team" by Patrick Lencioni.

- **Local Libraries**: Libraries often host seminars or can connect you with local resources. They also have a range of books and materials available for self-study.

- **Podcasts and YouTube Channels**: There are many podcasts and YouTube channels dedicated to leadership, management, and personal development. They can be a great resource for learning on the go.

The bottom line is you need strong Executive Function to be able to get your business to the level you desire. Take a hard look at how you behave and what needs work for you to get both yourself and the business to the next level, then create a plan to build the skills you lack. Below is an assessment to help you find out what you need to work on to get better at Executive Functions.

EXECUTIVE FUNCTION ASSESSMENT

** *Here is an assessment I created for my coaching clients. We use it to quantify where each client is in terms of executive function and it is our guide to know what areas I need to help the client improve in.*

INSTRUCTIONS:

For each question, you'll select whether you agree, are neutral, or disagree. Each choice will have a point value. At the end of the quiz, tally your points to see where you stand.

Points:

Agree: 2 points

Neutral: 1 point

Disagree: 0 points

Procrastination on Important Decisions

I often delay making important business decisions, which can result in missed opportunities or rushed judgments.

- » Agree
- » Neutral
- » Disagree

Lack of Clear Business Goals

I do not have clearly defined, measurable goals for my business, making it hard to prioritize and allocate resources effectively.

- » Agree
- » Neutral
- » Disagree

Poor Time Management

I struggle with managing my time efficiently, often finding that critical tasks and opportunities are overlooked.

> » Agree

> » Neutral

> » Disagree

Difficulty in Delegating Tasks

I find it hard to delegate tasks, leading to overextension and potential neglect of strategic business opportunities.

> » Agree

> » Neutral

> » Disagree

Resistance to Change or New Ideas

I am hesitant to adopt new technologies or methods, potentially missing out on innovations that could benefit my business.

> » Agree

> » Neutral

> » Disagree

Inconsistent Financial Planning

I do not regularly review or adjust my business's financial plans, which can lead to missed opportunities for investment or growth.

> » Agree

> » Neutral

> » Disagree

Neglecting Market Research

I infrequently conduct market research, which may result in missed opportunities to adapt to market trends or customer needs.

» Agree

» Neutral

» Disagree

Underestimating the Importance of Customer Engagement

I do not prioritize customer engagement and feedback, missing opportunities to improve service quality and customer loyalty.

» Agree

» Neutral

» Disagree

Failing to Invest in Employee Development

I overlook the importance of investing in my employees' development, which could lead to a more skilled but overlooked workforce.

» Agree

» Neutral

» Disagree

Not Utilizing Data for Business Decisions

I rarely use data analysis to inform my business decisions, potentially overlooking insights that could guide more effective strategies.

» Agree

» Neutral

» Disagree

Questions:

- Procrastination on Important Decisions
- Lack of Clear Business Goals
- Poor Time Management
- Difficulty in Delegating Tasks
- Resistance to Change or New Ideas
- Inconsistent Financial Planning
- Neglecting Market Research
- Underestimating the Importance of Customer Engagement
- Failing to Invest in Employee Development
- Not Utilizing Data for Business Decisions

Total Points: _____ (out of 20)

Scoring Interpretation:

0-6 Points: High Efficiency

You're likely managing your executive functions efficiently, minimizing opportunity costs. Keep up the good work and continue seeking ways to improve.

7–13 Points: Moderate Efficiency

You have some awareness of executive function's impact but could benefit from more focused attention in certain areas. Identifying and addressing these can significantly reduce opportunity costs.

14–20 Points: Opportunity for Improvement

Your responses suggest that executive function challenges may be leading to significant opportunity costs. Consider strategies for improving in areas like planning, delegation, and decision-making to enhance your business's efficiency and growth potential.

RECAP AND ACTION ITEMS

Like many of us, I struggle with executive function. I am creative and love coming up with unique ideas to work on, but it requires having the skills of executive function, the "adult" things in life, to make those visions and dreams a reality. Like many entrepreneurs, you may find that while you possess some of these skills, others will need to be consciously developed as you grow into your leadership role.

- **Implementation:** Dreams are wonderful, but they don't become reality through wishful thinking. It's the execution that counts. It's easy to get caught up in the creative aspects of business planning, like envisioning the perfect logo or branding strategy. However, the true essence of a successful business lies in taking those ideas and translating them into actions that drive progress and growth.

- **Emotional Control:** As a leader, maintaining emotional stability is key to fostering a trusting and effective team environment. We've all experienced the impact of working with emotionally volatile leaders, and it's not something I want for my team. Staying calm and consistent helps everyone stay engaged and confident in their roles, even during challenging times.

- **Focus and People Skills:** As your business evolves, it's essential to sharpen your focus and improve your delegation skills. Letting go of day-to-day tasks to concentrate on strategic planning can be difficult, but it's necessary for sustainable growth. Moreover, cultivating strong interpersonal skills is crucial for building a cohesive team and maintaining positive client relationships.

By embracing and enhancing these skills, you're not just driving your business forward; you're also creating a more supportive and fulfilling work environment.

ACTION ITEMS:

- **Set Clear, Actionable Goals:** I make it a practice to break down my big visions into manageable, actionable tasks. Whether it's refining my marketing strategy, choosing the right consultants, or making key hires, I ensure that each step is purposeful and directly contributes to our growth.

- **Practice Emotional Awareness:** I've found tools like the DISC assessment incredibly helpful in understanding my emotional triggers and reactions. I take time to reflect on my responses and give myself space to think before reacting, ensuring that all my interactions are respectful and constructive.

- **Delegate with Trust:** Learning to trust my team with significant responsibilities has not only lightened my own workload but has also empowered them. This builds a strong sense of ownership and teamwork. At the same time, I focus on developing my leadership and interpersonal skills to better guide my team and deepen our client relationships.

SECTION 2:
THE BUSINESS

AS WE ROLLED OUT NEW
SYSTEMS IT BECAME
APPARENT THAT WE
COULD NOT BEGIN
IMPLEMENTATION OF
THE NEXT SYSTEM UNTIL
THE PRIOR WAS DONE BY
EVERYONE CONSISTENTLY.

CHAPTER 4:

THE IMPORTANCE OF SYSTEMS

As I sat at my desk one morning after our daily huddle, I listened in as my office team and some senior technicians tried to explain to a new employee all the steps required to take a dump trailer to the dump for disposal. Now, that probably seems like a fairly normal occurrence at many businesses. However, I had heard this same song and dance about taking trash to the dump a hundred times over the years, and this time it was making my blood boil. I was not mad at my team, but mad at myself for not having created systems for my business years ago. Instead of doing the work and taking the time to build proper systems so my business would run smoothly, I chose to ignore the issue and live in a business full of chaos, inefficiency, and frustration for all of us who worked there. It was time to change.

After they sorted out the new team member and got him situated to do his first dump run, I called in my office manager to talk to her about our need to finally build the system we needed and to create a plan of implementation. It was going to start with a written system of how to go to the dump! From that point, we were going to identify our biggest problems first and create systems to fix those headaches and after that, we would fill in all the blanks and complete systems for every business function. She was all in because she was so sick and tired of having to explain things over and over again to the team. It was time to build systems for the sake of our business and everyone in it.

The sad part of this is that I knew full well that we needed systems and why. I had read Michael Gerber's E-Myth, which is all about creating a systems-run business as opposed to a people-run business. My coach, Howard Partridge, was always encouraging me to implement systems for all we did within the business. So, it was not as if I did not understand how important systems were or how to create them. The problem was me. It was a daunting task to sit down and write down exactly how to do every single task in our business. Where would I begin? How long will this take? Will people even use the systems once I make them? Do I need to do all of this myself? Am I even smart enough to do this?

I was paralyzed with fear. It seemed like too much, so I stuck my head in the sand for far too long and just worked in a reactive, inefficient, people-driven company that could no longer grow because we had no systems. I was the bottleneck for our success.

Using my annoyance with the dump run drama as fuel for change, I started there. The next day, my office manager, armed with a notebook and her iPhone, walked through every aspect of the dump run with one of my senior technicians. She took photos, and videos, created a map, and a full step-by-step process flow to complete a successful dump run. The next morning, she presented me with a small 3-ring binder with pictures, maps, and instructions to successfully complete every single aspect of this task with zero help from anyone else in the organization. In two hours, she fixed a problem that had plagued us for years. To test out her new creation, we sent our newest and least experienced employee to the dump armed with only the new dump run binder. Within the hour, he was back at the shop having completed the dump run with no issues and no help from any other team members. I was now officially addicted to creating systems.

I learned then and there how crucial having a system for everything was to our business. This lit a fire in me to build as many systems as possible to try to have a procedure for everything that happened in our business. But here is the rub, you will never be done building and implementing systems. As your business grows, changes, and evolves, you will always be tweaking, adding, and subtracting systems in your business. The better you can do this, the faster you can grow your business to the coveted mark.

Ok, Eric, this all sounds great but how do I do this and where do I start?

We started to work on building systems as a team exercise. The key element of implementing systems (and I cannot stress this enough) is how important it was to include the team in building our systems. People generally don't like change. Even less do they like management and ownership dictating how to do their jobs. We needed buy-in from the team and to do that I needed to sell them on "why" we needed systems and what the benefit was for them by doing this. So, we had several meetings talking about why systems are so important, how we should build and implement our new systems, and most importantly I explained what was in it for them and I asked for their help to make this happen. Without them, I said, there was no way we could pull this off. Beyond the team's input and expertise, I needed them to be a big part of our system building. I needed them to help create our new systems culture because without their help we were never going to be able to implement the changes necessary to build a business that would be better for all of us.

Once we got team buy-in, we hatched a plan. I headed up the project with my office manager to figure out what systems needed to be created and in what order. We would sit down with various managers and technicians to help us create a system for everything. Then, I would create a system and process flow for each task. We would then give the new system to the team members for two weeks for their input and changes that needed to be made. After that, we came up with a final system and it was to be implemented every day from that point forward. A key thing we learned was to not rush the implementation phase for each new system. People had become accustomed to doing things the "old way" and it took some time to get used to doing the new, best-practice system. As we rolled out new systems, it became very apparent that we could not begin implementation of the next system until the one prior was done by everyone consistently. Systems building is easy. Systems implementation is a much slower process and a lot of patience and training is required.

The way we began to build the systems out was to work through every aspect of our business. Here is a brief and incomplete list of the things we worked on. This is for you to see the thought process we went through as we began system-building. Here was our basic process:

OUR IMPLEMENTATION MAP

Customer Relationship Management (CRM)

First, we needed a CRM system that would be robust enough to handle our business not only in its current state but powerful enough to grow with us as we grew. Once we identified the right software for our needs, we needed to get everyone comfortable with using it. So we began a series of checklists for each department in our company on how to train them. Here is what it looked like:

Admin Team:

- Understand the CRM's interface and navigation. Just get a basic understanding of how to use it.

- Set up user accounts and permissions.

- Import and manage customer data from our old CRM.

- Configure service offerings, pricing, and inventory. *(Build our Price List)*

- Familiarize the team with reporting tools for performance analysis. *(Build KPIs)*

Customer Service Representatives (CSRs):

- Learn how to create and manage customer profiles.

- Master appointment scheduling and dispatching. *(This takes a lot of training and practice. You can make or lose a lot of money here, so the owner's involvement is often needed.)*

- Utilize communication tools (e.g., email, texting, Slack) for customer interactions.

- Understand billing and invoicing processes. *(CSRs get lots of billing questions and should have a basic understanding of how it all works to help them answer some questions.)*

- Handle service requests, cancellations, and rescheduling.

- Troubleshoot common customer issues within the CRM.

- Practice effective note-taking and documentation. *(We always worked on having great documentation. It fixes a lot of internal problems.)*

Managers:

- Gain proficiency in generating and interpreting reports.

- Monitor team performance metrics and KPIs *(Key Performance Indicators).*

- Implement strategies to optimize scheduling and resource allocation.

- Develop protocols for handling angry clients and customer feedback.

Field Technicians:

- Install and familiarize themselves with the CRM mobile app on their phones and iPads.

- Access job details, including customer information and service requirements. *(We practiced doing this on a big screen TV together to show everyone how it's done.)*

- Update job statuses, progress notes, and completed tasks in real-time.

- Utilize in-app communication tools to collaborate with CSRs and Managers.

- Capture customer signatures and complete necessary forms electronically.

Once we got all squared away with our CRM, we started tackling our scheduling and booking system. We realized we could either make much more money or potentially spend far too much by how we scheduled and booked jobs. Therefore, creating a solid system and rules about how to schedule and book was crucial. I cannot tell you how many afternoons I spent with my admin team and CSR team's brainstorming and fine-tuning sessions to get the maximal production out of each day from the field production team.

Here are the things we worked on to dial in our scheduling to max out our daily revenue and still not overload our techs with too much drive time and the stress of Los Angeles traffic:

Route Optimization: We planned our technicians' routes as efficiently as possible to minimize travel time and the distance between jobs. We found some route optimization software to automatically generate the most efficient routes based on the locations of the day's appointments. We also spend a lot of time with the CSRs and the dispatchers to book client's jobs by city so we could have minimal commute time. For non-emergency work, this was pretty easy, but for our water damage emergency response teams, this was never going to be perfect.

Group Jobs by Location: We created systems and scripts to group jobs that are in close proximity to each other together. Instead of the CSRs asking the client, "What days are good for you?" we scripted how to offer them multiple options of dates and times based on where we already had jobs. This reduces travel time between jobs and allows technicians to complete more jobs in a shorter amount of time.

Schedule Full Days: I hated to see guys back at the shop at 2 p.m. with nothing to do and then I either needed to send them home or burn profit with shop time. To overcome this, we created systems to schedule each van for a full day of work whenever possible. This avoided gaps in the schedule that left technicians with idle time between appointments. A big change for us to eliminate this problem was to have longer arrival time schedules that overlapped. This was a game changer for us monetarily. The CSRs were worried about this at the beginning. However, we created a script and role-played with them to help them overcome booking window fears.

Optimize Technician Productivity: We realized we had done a very poor job of making sure our technicians had the necessary tools, equipment, and training to complete jobs efficiently. To eliminate this, we implemented morning and evening checklists for every van to make sure techs were not calling in from the field saying they did not have this or that. To make sure the checklists were done correctly each morning, the admin team and the managers would conduct a lineup of all vans and double-check their checklists before they could drive to the first job. Systems like this can save you thousands and thousands of dollars in gained efficiency. We also implemented a 3 p.m. phone meeting with all managers to get a status update on each job. By doing this, we could make crucial decisions in real time about pulling one team to go help out at a big job or deciding to eat a few hours of overtime and have a team stay on a job late to finish instead of going back the next day. The 3 p.m. meeting system was one of the best ideas our team ever came up with to drive efficiency.

Field Procedures: For most home service businesses, the majority of issues that rear their ugly head happen in the field. Also, I have found lack of systems and proper technician training usually lie at the heart of most fires you need to put out. So the next time you get really angry with a field technician for not doing it your way or how he/she was supposed to do it, ask yourself: *did I have a solid system in place for this and, if so, have I consistently trained my team on how to do it? The answer is rarely yes.*

That said, building field systems should be one of the easier tasks for most home service owners, as they started their business out in the field doing the work. Yet, it rarely ever gets done. What gets to a lot of us is our impatience, so we just do it ourselves. We have never slowed down long enough to write out each step. It takes a lot of mental energy to write down each and every step in a linear, process-flow style. However, if you never take the time to do this, you will never be able to grow much bigger than the amount of work you can be personally involved in.

Let me give you an example of what I am talking about. I worked tirelessly with my operations teams to come up with documents like the one below. We would work together to come up with each step we needed to perform correctly every single action our company did in the field. The image below is a process flow for a new water damage job. Our lead technicians and project managers would work off this checklist to ensure each and every step was completed so there were no mistakes and oversights on jobs.

As you will see from this checklist, we walk the employee step by step with short instructions to make sure that he/she does every step of the job as needed. It is common for team members to create their own systems in the absence of the ones created for them, so be sure your systems work. If not, everyone will continue to do it in their own way.

Water Damage Job Management Checklist		
Item to Complete	**Date**	**Emp.**
Locate source and stop water flowing.		
Create scope of work and shoot video for adjuster explaining loss in detail.		
Find out who **OWNS** property and contact them for insurance claim info		
Get contract signed and in your possession by **OWNER**		
Explain timeline, scope of work, and what is going to happen to owner (occupant). **Don't sugarcoat anything and do not be vague.** Tell them what needs to happen. Be nice, but be in control. This is your job, you need to take charge.		
Do work necessary to begin. If building built prior to 1985 call John Doe at ABC Environmental for lead and asbestos testing. Cell: 123-456-7890		
If tests come back positive for lead and/or asbestos, call Jane Smith with XYZ Abatement for removal of the materials. She can be reached at 987-765-4321.		
Once demo is done by ABC or our company. Place equipment and dry out structure. Have client sign equipment form.		
Keep a file of every item used and every hour worked. Also, keep an updates moisture map for proof of insurance.		
Call homeowner and/or occupant **EVERY DAY** during dry out to make sure they are ok and that they know what is going on.		
Day 2 call		
Day 3 call		
Day 4 call		
Day 5 call		
When dry, shoot video for adjuster showing dry readings and what was done.		
Pull Equipment		
Get Certificate of Satisfaction signed by **OWNER**.		
Finish scope using files, Company Cam, and Albiware		
Review scope with lead technician for accuracy		
Review scope carefully, do change order if necessary.		
Send scope into insurance company for payment.		
Mitigation Manager deals with carrier regarding scope changes (if necessary)		
Office stays in contact with carrier to see when check will be sent.		
Deposit Check and Close out file		

Depending on your software, these process flows can obviously be created digitally. It is best to have everything available digitally so every employee who needs access can work from the same file and process flow. There are also wonderful tools that are now available to help business owners create systems and process flows.

Once you get a handle on what systems you need to build and how to build them, the actual hard (and most frustrating) part begins—getting everyone to actually use the systems every time. This was a real struggle for me. Once I got going, my managers and I could crank out systems and process flows pretty quickly. However, getting 100 percent compliance from the staff was always a challenge. People get stuck in their ways and often like to do things the way they have always done them in the past. The trick I learned as I put systems in place was to only implement one new system at a time. I'd never move off implementing it until everyone is doing it the new way every single time. This can be so painstaking and frustrating, especially for hard-charging entrepreneurs who want action and results. Trust me, slow down and take a breath—do not implement the next system until the one you are implementing now is being used all of the time.

RECAP AND ACTION ITEMS

The contents of this chapter were a reflection of a pivotal moment in my business journey, sparked by an everyday task: a routine explanation to a new employee about how to handle a dump run. It sounds simple, yet it served as a crucial wake-up call for me. The repetitive nature of this task and the realization of underlying inefficiencies in our operations led me to a significant decision—to systematize our business processes. This wasn't just about fixing a process; it was about fundamentally changing how we operated to better create growth and efficiency.

ACTION ITEMS:

- **Start with the Basics:** My first step was to tackle a basic, yet essential task—the dump run. I chose this because it was a manageable process that every employee could relate to and see the immediate benefits of systematizing. We documented each step meticulously, which not only streamlined the task but also served as a model for systematizing other processes. It was about creating a template that could be replicated across the company, showing quick wins to motivate the team for more comprehensive changes.

- **Engage and Empower the Team:** One of the key lessons I learned early on was the importance of involving the entire team in this shift. This wasn't about handing down new rules from up high; it was about collaborative development of systems. We held workshops where team members could voice their challenges and suggestions. This approach not only improved the systems we were building but also ensured everyone felt invested in the success of these changes. Their direct involvement meant they were more likely to embrace and adhere to the new systems.

- **Implement with Care and Patience:** The temptation to implement all systems at once was strong, but experience taught me that a gradual rollout was more effective. We introduced each new system carefully, allowed time for everyone to adjust, and were open to feedback. This iterative process helped us fine-tune our systems without overwhelming the team. It also reinforced the idea that these changes were about continuous improvement, not just one-off adjustments.

This step-by-step approach not only reduced chaos and inefficiency but also set a foundation for scalable growth. By systematizing mundane tasks, we freed up resources and energy to focus on strategic goals. The journey of systematization taught me that true transformation requires patience, collaboration, and a willingness to adapt.

THE TWO THINGS WE HAVE
THE MOST CONTROL OVER
IS WHAT WE CHARGE FOR
THE WORK WE DO AND
HOW MUCH IT COSTS US
TO PERFORM THAT WORK.
THESE TWO VARIABLES
ARE AT THE HEART OF
JOB COSTING.

CHAPTER 5:
UNDERSTANDING YOUR FINANCIALS

I do not love accounting. In fact, in the early years of the business, I avoided looking at the numbers at all costs. I would check the bank account balance and how much payroll was going to be, and as long as there was some money left over, all was good. However, as the business began to grow, my "checking account" system of financial management no longer worked. I needed help. I knew there was one person we knew who understood what we needed to do—Ellen Rohr. Ellen Rohr is a force of nature. She is so much fun and super positive. Ellen makes doing your financials seem cool, and she never judges your financial position. She has been there and struggled just like the rest of us. She began as "the plumber's wife" trying to help her husband keep their plumbing company from sinking. Ellen sought out help and became a rock star in the world of home service finance. We were lucky enough to have Ellen coach us for a year to learn how to read and manage our finances. Ellen explained to me how to read and analyze a Profit and Loss statement and a Balance Sheet. Over time, Ellen fostered in me a love for looking at the books.

During the same time period, I was also introduced to Chuck Violand of Violand Management Associates. Chuck taught me to dig even deeper into my numbers and begin job costing each and every job to better understand my pricing, efficiency rates, and how to better manage the business by looking at financial data. These two amazing people changed my life and changed how I look at a business. I went from what Howard Partridge calls "Elvis Accounting" (if you are running out of money just get another gig) to being able to have a strong handle on my cash flow, my real cost of doing business, and what I needed to charge people to make sure I ran a healthy business. If I can do this, anyone can. Let's break down a few of the real-world financial tools you need to get comfortable with to grow your business to six figures and beyond.

Job Costing

Job costing serves many functions in a business, such as profitability analysis, accurate pricing of your goods and services, managing your teams for efficiency of work, budgeting and forecasting future jobs and contracts, and managing cash flow. As your business grows, it becomes more data-driven out of necessity. When your business is small and you are doing a lot of the work, you can absorb some inefficiency. As you grow and have a larger payroll expense, more vehicles, a bigger building, and larger marketing expenses, it becomes crucial to count every penny and run as efficiently as possible. This is where job costing factors in. In a home service business where labor is often the #1 expense, our ability to control our COGS (Cost of Goods Sold) is critical to our success. If you think about it in real-world terms, this becomes evident. We don't have much control over the cost of our building, utilities, business insurance, vans, and all the rest of our general overhead expenses. The two things we have the most control over are what we charge for the work we do and how much it costs us to perform that work. These two variables are at the heart of job costing.

I have the good fortune to work with many home services companies each day through the consulting division of my company, Super Tech University. In this function, I coach owners and managers to run their businesses more deliberately with the use of data. The first question I ask every company I work with is: *Are you job costing?* I have yet to get any small business owners to tell me that they do. This is one of the tragedies of the small business world. I cannot stress this enough. We all need to job cost to keep our COGS in line with our pricing.

Below is a sample of a job costing sheet we used in our carpet cleaning business.

Name: Date/Time:

Category	Begin	End
Drive TIme		
Gas Level		
Job Mileage		
On Job TIme		
Truckmount Hours		

Type	Square Footage	Production Rate/Hour*

Product	Amount	Cost*

Employees	Total Time (Travel/Work)	Total Cost*

Office Use Only Below Line

Money In	Money Out	Violand Profit Target #	Percentage (P/L)	Happy/Cad

As you look over this job costing sheet, you will likely see a few things that might not make sense to you. You will see the "Violand Profit Target #" box which was based on the numbers I learned from Chuck Violand. Based on our expenses on the job, which needed to be at 40 percent (or lower) of the money we brought in, we could calculate the real price we needed to get on any given job to make at least 60 percent gross profit. This number was our goal for the job.

You also see a "Happy/Sad" box on the far right. The admin team would draw a smiley face or a frowny face on that box to indicate whether we made our goal or not. It was our fun way to track the data. It also signaled them to make a note in our CRM that we needed to discuss this job in the near future to figure out what went wrong. Did we under-bid the job? Were there extenuating circumstances on the job? Did our team work too slow and lose time? This is how job costing can change your effectiveness and hold everyone involved with a job accountable for doing good work.

Revenue Per Employee

Job costing is a wonderful tool that really helps you manage the productivity of your field staff and estimators, but revenue per employee is where the rubber meets the road. If there is one key metric that I want to know in my business, it is revenue per employee. This tells me if I am bringing in enough money to make sure I am profitable and lets me know if I am under – or over-staffed compared to industry averages.

For example, Apple has probably one of the highest revenue per employee numbers in the world. Here is how to figure out revenue per employee:

In Apple's 2022 Annual Report (Fiscal Year ended Sept 24, 2022):

Total Revenue: $394.3 billion

Total Employees: 164,000

Using these numbers, we can calculate an approximate revenue per employee of:

Revenue per Employee = Total Revenue / Total Employees

= $394.3 billion / 164,000 employees

= Approximately $2.4 million per employee

For a healthy HVAC company, that number may look like $350,000–$500,000 per employee. For a carpet cleaner where the tickets are smaller and the biggest expense is labor, that number may look like $125,000–$150,000 per employee. Every industry is different, but I feel it is important for every business owner to know what this number should be for them. Most industry associations or consultants could provide this number for you.

In a home service business, where labor is a significant component of the service provided, revenue per employee becomes supercritical. It helps in evaluating the effectiveness of your workforce in generating revenue and managing costs. Revenue per employee is a really great indicator of how well you are managing your company.

Here are a few things to consider as you begin to track this all-important metric:

- **Efficiency:** A higher revenue per employee indicates that each employee is generating more revenue, which can signify better efficiency and productivity. Conversely, a lower revenue per employee might suggest that your workforce is not operating at full capacity or that there are inefficiencies in your operations.

- **Tracking it as a KPI:** To track revenue per employee effectively as a key performance indicator (KPI), you need to:

  » *Regularly calculate and monitor it:* Calculate revenue per employee at regular intervals (e.g., monthly, quarterly) to track trends over time.

  » *Benchmark against industry standards:* Compare your revenue per employee with industry benchmarks to see how you stack up against competitors and identify areas for improvement.

> » *Drill down into factors influencing the metric:* Analyze factors such as employee productivity, service pricing, and operational efficiency to understand what drives changes in revenue per employee.

> » *Set targets and goals:* Use revenue per employee as a benchmark to set realistic targets and goals for your workforce. Encourage employees to strive for continuous improvement.

> » *Consider seasonality and external factors:* Take into account seasonal fluctuations and external factors that may impact revenue per employee, such as changes in market demand or economic conditions.

If you only do two things in this entire book, other than taking better care of yourself so you can be a high performer, please start job costing every job and track revenue per employee. These changed my whole business by making me face some hard truths and take action to become more efficient and profitable. Remember, everything measured improves.

YOUR FINANCIAL MAP: PROFIT & LOSS STATEMENT AND BALANCE SHEET

Until I committed to hiring a part-time bookkeeper and looking at the P&L and Balance Sheet on a weekly basis, I did not fully understand my business's finances. I was not able to make quick adjustments when spending was rising or make informed decisions on future purchases and the true health of the company. Ellen Rohr helped me understand these concepts and, more than anything, got me to understand that I was no longer "just a technician" but also a business owner. Business owners learn to consistently watch their finances. So I am going to defer to Ellen here to explain the importance of why you need to learn about the P&L and Balance Sheet. Ellen emphasizes the importance of breaking down financial concepts into simple terms so that even those without a financial background can understand them.

Profit and Loss (P&L) Statement:

She often refers to the P&L as the "report card" for how a business is doing over a certain period (e.g., monthly, quarterly, yearly). It shows revenues (sales), costs of goods sold, operating expenses, and the resulting profit or loss for the given period.

Ellen stresses the importance of regularly reviewing this statement to understand if the business is making money.

Balance Sheet:

Ellen describes the Balance Sheet as a snapshot of a company's financial position at a specific point in time. It lists the assets (what the company owns), liabilities (what the company owes), and equity (the difference between assets and liabilities). Ellen points out that while the P&L shows how well you are doing, the Balance Sheet shows how much you have and how much owe.

KPIs: Key Performance Indicators

One of the brightest minds in the home service space is A1 Garage's Tommy Mello. I have met Tommy a few times and he has been a guest on my Blue Collar Nation Podcast. I saw Tommy give a keynote speech recently and he did a deep dive on KPIs. Tommy stated that he felt he could run almost any business with 4 key KPIs.

1. Average Ticket: The average amount of each sold job
2. Face-to-Face Conversion Rate: The percentage of proposals that turned into jobs by a tech
3. Booking Rate: The percentage of calls turned into estimates
4. Cost Per Acquisition: The amount of money it took to get the job sold

Let's look into this a little deeper to discuss why these 4 are so important and how to read into what they mean and how to manage it.

First, let's start with what we can learn from booking rates. This allows us to examine the number of phone calls coming into our business.

This indicates whether our marketing efforts are paying off—do we bring in enough potential work to grow our business? It holds our customer service representatives (CSR) accountable for getting the caller to agree to allow one of our estimators or technicians to come to their home or business to do an inspection.

Second, face-to-face conversion rates tell us how good our front-line team members are doing in sales and turning inspections into paying jobs.

Third, the average ticket gives us a great sense of how good we are at sales and whether we are charging enough to successfully run our business. If the average tickets are low, it is often a cue that we need to invest the time and resources to make sure our team members are confident and competent salespeople.

Last, cost per acquisition digs into how we are getting our work and whether we are overpaying for the leads. This KPI gives us the information we need to make sure our marketing approach is on point and sustainable.

There are obviously many more KPIs to consider in a business than the ones listed above. The point I am trying to make is that business is becoming more data-driven and there are many tools to help you with the quantitative analysis of your home service business. None of us can ignore this trend. As private equity firms enter every home services marketplace in the country, we cannot afford to ignore these new trends. It would be at our peril.

If you are competing with home services businesses that have taken private equity investment, you are no longer competing against your local plumber or electrician. You are now competing with Ivy League MBAs who run that business by the numbers. They collect data and make decisions accordingly. The good news is you can learn how to do this, too. Combine that with your local knowledge, trade skills, and service mindset and you can compete with anyone.

RECAP AND ACTION ITEMS

In the beginning, I was all about keeping things simple in my business. I avoided the deep dive into our numbers like it was a chore I could forever dodge. My method was what you might call "Elvis Accounting"—if money was tight, just drum up some more work. However, as the business began to scale up, this seat-of-the-pants financial management was no longer cutting it. I needed a lifeline, and that's when Ellen Rohr came into the picture.

Ellen, with her infectious energy and straightforward approach, made finance seem not only manageable but actually cool. She helped me shift my view from just checking the bank balance to truly understanding what the numbers were telling me. Under her guidance, I learned to read and analyze Profit & Loss statements and Balance Sheets. This wasn't just about keeping the business afloat anymore; it was about planning for growth and stability.

Chuck Violand was another game changer for me. He taught me to dig deeper, to really dissect the numbers through job costing. Every single job became a case study in pricing, efficiency, and management. This level of detail in our financial analysis wasn't just about keeping score; it was about refining our operations and becoming more competitive.

Both Ellen and Chuck transformed my approach to business. From flying blind, I moved to a data-driven strategy, utilizing financial tools and insights that allowed me to not just understand but also predict and control my business dynamics.

ACTION ITEMS:

- **Embrace Job Costing Rigorously:** Start job costing every single project. This isn't just a financial exercise—it's about gaining insights into every aspect of your operations. Understand how much each job should cost versus how much it does cost. This helps you refine your pricing models and improve your bottom line.

- **Adopt Revenue Per Employee as a Key Metric:** This metric transformed how I view workforce productivity. Regularly track and analyze revenue per employee to ensure each team member's output aligns with your business goals. It's a straightforward metric that provides deep insights into operational efficiency and financial health.

- **Commit to Regular Financial Reviews:** Engage deeply with your financial statements. Schedule weekly reviews of your Profit & Loss Statement and Balance Sheet. This habit gives you a clearer understanding of your financial status and helps you make informed decisions quickly. It's not just about knowing your current position, but about actively shaping your business's future through informed strategic planning.

By adopting these practices, you can shift from being reactive in your financial management to being strategically proactive, setting your business on a path to sustainable growth and profitability.

SO WHAT DOES REFERRAL MARKETING LOOK LIKE? WELL, IT LOOKS LIKE WORK! IT TAKES SOMEONE IN YOUR COMPANY TO GO OUT INTO THE BUSINESS COMMUNITY AND MEET PEOPLE.

CHAPTER 6:
LOCAL BOOTS ON THE GROUND MARKETING

When I first opened my home service business, I had no idea I would have to get out there and market face to face by knocking on doors. At the time the phone book and the newspaper were the main ways to market a service business. Being the introvert that I am, I figured I could just pay to get work and not have to ever go door to door to market my business. The reason this was so important to me was that I was terrified to go knock on a door and actually talk to strangers. You see, like many of you reading this book, I loved to go out in the field and do the work, but I hated the idea of having to sell myself to get the work. However, it became very obvious to me that my phone was not going to just ring and I needed to build up the courage to go door to door and meet people so I could tell them how great our company was.

I will never forget that first day of knocking on doors. I sat in my car sweating and procrastinating to go hand out flyers. I was scared shitless that people would yell at me, kick me out of their offices, be rude to me. I thought I was going to throw up and even considered just quitting my business in that moment. However, I mustered up the courage to go knock on some doors and you know what? Nobody yelled at me. Nobody kicked me out of their offices. Nobody was even rude to me. I thought, that wasn't so bad. What have I been so worried about? All I needed to do was be nice, be respectful of them and their time, make a quick introduction, and get out of there. I was now on my way to becoming a real door-to-door marketer.

There are a few ways to grow most home service businesses. There is what I will refer to as referral marketing and digital marketing. One of these subjects I feel very proficient in (referrals), the other is digital marketing. For that reason, I will speak about marketing here and devote a standalone section to digital marketing by my friend and marketing guru, Katie Harris of Spot On Solutions Marketing. Katie has been my go-to person for digital marketing when I owned my disaster restoration and cleaning business and Spot on Solutions still does all digital marketing for my company, Super Tech University. I, on the other hand, now feel very comfortable talking to you about referral marketing.

REFERRAL AND LOCAL MARKETING

I use the term referral marketing for all aspects of marketing with people in your local community. Finding companies and local people who refer your business to others is how we grow our business within our community. However, how we make this happen can take many forms.

To grow your service business to six figures and beyond, you need a lot of local people cheering you on and wanting your company to be a success. To get recognized in the community, you need to be an active participant in the local business scene. As important as digital marketing is to be successful in today's marketplace, any good digital marketing expert will also tell you that you need multiple ways to market your business. It is important to pair local referral marketing and digital marketing together.

So what does local referral marketing look like? Well, it looks like work! It takes someone in your company to go out into the business community and meet people. Here are a few of the ways my company used local referral marketing to grow our service business.

CHAMBER OF COMMERCE

The local chamber of commerce is an excellent place to grow a local network of referral partners. Every chamber has various events each month where you get to highlight your company and get to know other professionals who can feed your company work. Chambers worked so well at my company for creating referral relationships—we were active members of five chambers of commerce in the areas where we did the most work. However, chambers take time and effort. I often hear people say they joined a chamber and never got any work from it. You cannot just join a chamber and get work. You will get out of a chamber what you are willing to put into it. Go to the events, become an ambassador, get on the board of directors. You have to work hard to get what you want. You also need to view your chamber membership as an opportunity to give. Companies that don't refer chamber members will not receive referrals from other chamber members. Become part of your chamber community and it will be the gift that keeps on giving and giving.

LOCAL COMMUNITY SERVICE GROUPS

Another way to get referrals is to join local community groups such as Kiwanis, Rotary, Lions Club, just to name a few. There are also many local charity groups in every town where many business owners are active participants in the communities where their businesses are located. Become involved in a group that speaks to your beliefs and company culture. I became involved in a local Kiwanis club not only to meet other local business people but also to get involved in doing charity work for underprivileged children. I got to make a difference in people's lives in my community. I met and did business with many like-minded business owners who were also Kiwanis members. In fact, my Kiwanis group was a top-performing referral source in our business for many years. Although it was not a business group and I was explicitly told to never market my company to the group, I didn't need to. I got to know many other business owners in that group and we all passed referrals to each other because we knew, liked, and trusted each other.

BUSINESS GROUPS

Another way to get referrals is to join and be active in a business group. Groups such as BNI (Business Network International), EO (Entrepreneurs Organization), and any local leads group that may exist in your town. You need to carefully consider each group before joining. Are there other members who can refer you? Can you refer others in the group? Is the time they meet conducive to your work schedule?

I have been a member of a BNI group for more than a decade. Much like a chamber of commerce, you will get into a leads group what you put into it. Make sure to go to the meetings, participate, find potential referral partners, and ask them for a lunch or coffee meeting to see how you can pass each other work.

Referral Marketing Routes

Going door-to-door and marketing your services to other companies is not very high on most people's lists of a good time. Many home service business owners will avoid doing door-to-door marketing at all costs but it would be to their detriment. Creating marketing routes and consistently visiting potential referral partners is a great way to grow your home service business. I can speak from experience that marketing this way can work wonders for your business and catapult you toward that business.

In my service company, referral route marketing was our #1 way to grow our business. In our disaster restoration and cleaning business, we targeted a few industries that could refer us again and again. They were plumbing companies, property management companies, and insurance agents. To get to know these companies, we set up monthly marketing routes to visit them, bring them some food and swag, and get to know the people there. We wanted to be on top of their minds any time they were referring out those services. Simple, but not easy.

Success is rarely easy—it is those companies who will do what others are unwilling to do that often succeed the most. We wanted to be a company willing to go the extra mile. Therefore, my business partner (and as we grew, several other team members, myself included) worked on a series of marketing stops each month where our goal was to earn trust and create a referral partnership. In our industry, one good plumbing shop could yield us hundreds of thousands if not millions of dollars in revenue per year. We took referral marketing very seriously and so should you.

A Plan for Going Door to Door:

It is not at all natural for many of us to go knock on doors and talk to strangers. As I recounted at the beginning of this chapter, I was so scared to go door to door. To make myself more comfortable doing it, I created lots of systems to make sure I was doing the best I could and also hold myself accountable for actually doing it each week. Let me share some of my systems for going door to door to, hopefully, make you feel more at ease getting out there and letting people know how great your company is.

The Secret Weapon:

I learned that food was my secret weapon against people being upset or annoyed with me. Food became like a shield from negative experiences. I would always be sure to enter every new door with some nice edible gift to give to the office. Nobody yells at the person bringing goodies! I would go to a store like Traders Joe's and find low-cost, but nice food items to take with me. Note: if you are going to do this and live in a hot climate, be sure to put your food items in a cooler so they don't melt in a hot car while you drive around to visit potential clients. There is nothing more embarrassing than delivering chocolates only to hear on your next visit they were all melted!

Afternoon Pick-Me-Up:

I used to love taking an afternoon caffeine fix to my potential clients. I would buy the wine-carrying cases that held four bottles of wine in bulk. I would then slap a sticker with my company logo on the carrying case and fill it up with cold Starbucks drinks, Red Bulls, Green Tea, and items that clients might like in the afternoon. My pick-me-up visits were a big hit and always got a lot of positive attention.

Signature Gift:

My business partner, Larry, is widely known for taking pineapples to his marketing stops. It stood out and Larry was often just referred to as the "Pineapple Guy" by many clients. However, Larry's idea was great because he stood out from all the rest of the marketers who were visiting potential referral sources. Nobody forgets the guy who shows up with a pineapple every time. In fact, Larry would even dress the pineapples up: a Santa hat at Christmas, rabbit ears at Easter, and an American flag for the 4th of July. Larry's signature gift made our company millions and millions of dollars over the years.

Promotional Materials:

We never visited without "leaving materials." We handed out business cards, full-page flyers, tri-folds, and other printed goods. We also liked to give out promotional items with our logo and contact information that would stay on people's desks and be a constant reminder that we existed. We handed out large plastic cups they could use at the water cooler, chip clips, pens, and pads of paper. We even gave our letter openers that included our business card inserted in the handle. We wanted to make sure they never forgot who we were.

Activity Tracking:

It's great to go marketing, but the key to success is volume (for the right targets) and being consistent. Nothing takes the place of getting out there and visiting potential partners on a monthly basis. Our business was built on consistently getting to our existing and potential referral partners EVERY month. In fact, to make sure I was being honest with myself I created this tracker I used for years to keep myself accountable for making my stops, phone calls, meetings, and texting.

Here is my sheet, feel free to tweak, digitize, or do whatever you need to do to this system to make it work for you:

Stops

OOOOOOOOOO
OOOOOOOOOO
OOOOOOOOOO
OOOOOOOOOO

Run Losses

OOOOO

Calls

OOOOOOOOOO

Meetings

OOO

Name	Date	Notes

I used this basic sheet in a 3-ring binder for years to track my daily activity. I wanted to make sure I was visiting enough businesses, calling enough people, and just doing enough activity to be a success. So much of the effectiveness of doing door-to-door local marketing is just the act of getting out there and communicating with people.

CRM AND FOLLOW-UP:

I used my paper sheet to track my progress quickly while I was going door to door, but I would input my stops into our CRM (Client Relations Management system) once I got back home each night. That way I could create notes and reminders of all the follow-ups I needed to do to make sure I was getting clients the information they needed while being sure to add value where I could. Please remember: THE MONEY IS IN THE FOLLOW-UP! You can't just visit and not continue to engage the people you visit. Send snail mail cards and letters, send emails, text them, make a phone call when applicable. The more you engage the people you visit, the more chance of getting their work you have. To do that effectively, you need to keep detailed notes and reminders to follow up.

CHECKLIST OF ITEMS YOU WILL NEED:

Basic Essentials:

- *Business Cards*: Professional, easy-to-read business cards with contact information

- *Brochures/Flyers*: Informative brochures or flyers detailing services offered, including benefits and customer testimonials

- *Referral Program Details*: Clear information about the referral program, including incentives for businesses that refer clients

- *Appointment Scheduler*: A portable scheduling tool, either a physical planner or a digital app, to set up follow-up meetings

- *Company Branded Materials*: Pens, notepads, and other small branded items that can be left behind as a reminder

Digital Tools:

- *Tablet or Smartphone*: To show digital presentations, capture contact information, and demonstrate the company's online presence

- *Customer Relationship Management (CRM) App*: To track interactions, follow-ups, and manage relationships with businesses

- *Email Templates*: Pre-written follow-up and thank you emails to send after visits

- *Social Media Information*: Easy access to the company's social media profiles to show the online presence and engagement

Marketing Collateral:

- *Case Studies*: Real-life examples of successful jobs and satisfied customers to build credibility

- *Testimonials*: Printed or digital testimonials from other businesses or customers

- *Service Packages*: Clear descriptions of service packages and pricing options

Personal Preparedness:

- *Professional Attire*: Dress appropriately to make a positive first impression

- *Knowledge of Services*: In-depth knowledge about all services offered to answer questions confidently

- *Local Knowledge*: Familiarity with the area and understanding of local businesses' needs and challenges

- *Polished Pitch*: A well-practiced, concise pitch that clearly explains the value proposition

Follow-up Strategy:

- *Follow-up Plan*: A clear plan for following up with businesses, including timelines and methods (calls, emails, visits)

- *Networking Strategy*: Tactics for building and maintaining relationships with local business owners and managers

- *Thank You Notes*: Personalized thank you notes to leave a lasting impression after meetings

RECAP AND ACTION ITEMS

In this chapter, I discussed effective strategies for growing home service businesses primarily through referral marketing, with an emphasis on the importance of integrating local community engagement into our marketing efforts. I share insights from my own experiences, focusing on the ways we can tap into local networks to establish a robust base of referrals. Here's a summary of the key points:

- **Referral Marketing in Local Communities:** I define referral marketing as actively engaging with local individuals and businesses to generate referrals within the community. This involves being a visible and contributing member of the local business scene, such as participating in the Chamber of Commerce and various community service groups (e.g., Kiwanis, Rotary). I emphasize the necessity of going beyond mere membership in these groups to gain meaningful business opportunities through genuine involvement and giving back.

- **Importance of Networking Groups:** I also discuss the importance of joining and being active in business networking groups like BNI (Business Network International) and local lead groups. These platforms offer avenues to meet potential referral partners, but they demand commitment and active participation. Building relationships based on mutual trust and reciprocity is crucial for securing reliable referrals.

- **Referral Marketing Routes:** I describe how we used marketing routes in my company as a direct strategy to engage potential referral partners such as plumbing companies, property management companies, and insurance agents. Regular visits to these businesses were key to establishing trust and rapport, which are essential for encouraging ongoing referrals.

ACTION ITEMS:

- **Engage Actively in Local Business Networks:** Join local chambers of commerce and participate in their events. Aim to become an integral part of these communities by taking on roles such as an ambassador or board member, which will enhance visibility and credibility.

- **Become Involved in Community Service Groups:** Identify and join community service groups that align with your company's values. Actively participate and contribute to these groups, which can lead to organic business referrals through shared community involvement and trust.

- **Establish and Maintain Marketing Routes:** Develop a structured approach to visit potential referral partners regularly. Focus on building genuine relationships by offering value, such as bringing gifts or useful items, to foster a connection that encourages these partners to refer your services naturally.

By integrating these strategies, businesses can create a diverse marketing approach that combines digital and referral marketing, leveraging local community engagement to drive growth and success.

WE WERE UNDER NO ILLUSION THAT WITHOUT SALES AND MARKETING AT THE FOREFRONT OF OUR BUSINESS, ALL OTHER ASPECTS WERE MEANINGLESS.

CHAPTER 7:
MAKING THE SALE

Once we get our marketing right and the phone starts ringing, we need to make sales. Many companies in the home service space are good at getting the phone to ring, but a lack of sales skills becomes a source of frustration. I know when I began my home services business, I had never sold a thing in my life. In fact, I grew up in a household where salespeople were held in very low regard. This made me nervous to "sell" to anyone. I didn't want to be perceived as the "slick used-car salesman" I had grown up watching characterized by television and movies.

I remember when I first started my air duct cleaning business I spent all of the start-up phase learning to do the technical work and zero time working my sales presentation skills. Big mistake. I was spending big bucks getting my phone to ring and not selling a darn thing. I quickly realized what my problem was and knew I had to fix it fast. I had a wife and two little girls to feed and shelter. No matter how I felt about sales, I needed to get good fast!

So, I did what any self-respecting entrepreneur would do—I took to the internet and found YouTube videos about sales. Then I purchased CDs for my truck, so I could role play out loud and learn to sell while I drove from bid to bid. Once I started to get some framework for what a sales process looked like, I tried out my new knowledge on clients and became better and better at sales. In fact, as the years passed and my confidence grew, in-home sales became my favorite thing to do. I realized sales was not a dirty word. I could not help people have better homes and better lives if I could not add value to them and give a good sales presentation.

As the years went on, my team and I were always on the lookout for new and better ways to ethically and honestly perform our sales training methods. As we grew, I sought out a coach to help me grow well past 7-figures. As I mentioned earlier, Howard Partridge had a profound influence on my life and my business. In fact, my company adopted Howard's 7-Step Sales Process for all of our estimators and technicians to use. The following is an outline of the 7-Step Sales Process from Howard's book, *The 5 Secrets to a Phenomenal Business:*

1. **Build Rapport**: This is about creating a connection with the potential customer. It involves being genuine, showing interest in them, and making them feel comfortable and understood.

2. **Qualify**: Before trying to sell something, it's important to ensure the potential customer actually needs or wants it. This step is about asking questions to understand their needs, desires, and pain points.

3. **Sell the Company**: Once you've identified a potential need, it's important to establish trust by selling the merits of your company. Why should they buy from you and not from someone else?

4. **Ask Questions**: This deepens the understanding of the customer's specific requirements, preferences, and constraints. The more you know, the better you can tailor your solution to them.

5. **Present the Solution**: Based on what you've learned, present your product or service as the solution to the customer's needs or problems. Highlight the benefits and how they address their specific requirements.

6. **Close the Sale**: This is the step where you ask for the commitment. Whether it's a signature, a deposit, or another form of agreement, this is when you finalize the transaction.

7. **Get Referrals**: After the sale, ask satisfied customers for referrals. This can lead to new business opportunities and help grow your network.

We used this system for years to build our multi-million dollar home service business. I would suggest getting a copy of Howard's book and really digging into the chapter on sales.

In addition to using Howard's book as our guide for creating a great sales process, we also felt that there was a need for some training and accountability to be added to the system to maximize its effectiveness. Here is what we added to create our full sales system:

Role Playing

To achieve the results we needed and wanted, our whole team needed to engage in consistent role-playing using the 7-Step Sales Process. I feel I need to let you in on a secret before I move forward about role play. My technicians and estimators hated it. Hell, I hated it. However, nothing works better for creating high-achieving sales teams than role-playing. Since none of us was particularly fond of doing it, we decided to make it fun and have a few laughs while improving our sales skills. We would make up scenarios for the tech to sell to. We would use past clients (especially the difficult ones) as the basis for the imaginary client. My techs got a hoot out of acting like our tougher clients and it really honed our skills when in front of new clients. Our sales conversion rates and average tickets went through the roof once we did weekly role-playing.

Public Accountability

Another key element I found to make us the best we could be at sales was some public accountability. I remembered how in high school, when I was a student-athlete, all the stats for every player were posted in the hallway for all the students to see. Nothing motivated me more than making sure I did well, so I would not have to take the ribbing of my peers when they read the latest batting average or scoring updates. So, in my business, we tracked all sales stats on a big whiteboard for all to see. As time went on and technology improved, we could display all data on big-screen TVs from information taken from our CRM.

Creating Process Flows and Sales Materials

My company specialized in emergency disaster restoration. Therefore, we never knew when and how much work was going to come in on any given day. When there were no weather events, we always had an estimator on hand to sell new jobs. However, when a storm would roll in, it was all hands on deck and often technicians were required to go sell when all of the estimators were busy. Because of this, we realized we needed sales materials that would walk both the customer and our technicians through our service offerings. In writing, we created a system for our techs to walk a client step by step through the entire sales process. We were blown away at how well this worked. The techs felt selling was easier for them by doing this and our estimators were so impressed with the process flows they implemented them into their sales process as well. Create a great communication tool to share with your clients and it will make the whole process of sales easier for your team.

Sales Training

Our mantra in my company was we are a sales and marketing company that happens to perform carpet cleaning and disaster restoration services. We were under no illusion that without sales and marketing at the fore-front of our business, all other aspects of the business were meaningless.

We needed strong sales to fund the growth we needed as a company and to provide opportunities for those working for us. This required a lot of training with the whole team to embrace this mindset and have the skills to deliver outstanding sales and marketing. I know earlier in this book, I referenced sales and suggested using Howard Partridge's 7-Point Sales Method. In this chapter, I want to impart to you how to get buy-in, what mental roadblocks your staff may have, and the practice methods to help them gain the skills they need.

Money Mindset

It has been my experience that many of your employees might have limiting beliefs about money. Hell, maybe you, the owner, have the same limiting beliefs. In order to sell anything to anyone, you need to get your mind right about money and abundance versus fear and scarcity. One cannot sell at a high level if their own fears and limiting beliefs are not addressed. I have seen time and time again how money issues can affect sales. Here is a list of some of the issues that are common occurrences during the sales process for those with money fears.

- **Projecting Personal Fears**: The salesperson might project their own financial anxieties onto the client. This means they might assume, often incorrectly, that the client is also worried about spending too much, leading them to hesitate in presenting more expensive options.

- **Underestimating Client's Buying Power**: Due to their own concerns about money, the salesperson might underestimate a client's buying power or willingness to spend. This can result in not offering higher-end products or services that the client might actually be interested in and capable of affording.

- **Hesitancy in Upselling or Cross-Selling**: Effective sales often involve upselling or cross-selling, where the salesperson encourages the client to purchase more expensive items or additional products. Money fears can make a salesperson less likely to engage in these practices, potentially missing out on larger sales.

- **Lack of Enthusiasm for High-Value Products**: If the salesperson is uneasy about the cost of certain items, they might lack enthusiasm when presenting these options. This lack of enthusiasm can be apparent to the client and may influence the client's perception of the value of these items.

- **Avoiding Discussions About Price**: A salesperson with money fears might avoid or feel uncomfortable discussing pricing, especially if the product or service is expensive. This can lead to a lack of clarity and potentially a missed opportunity if the client is actually open to higher-priced options.

- **Bias Toward Lower-Cost Solutions**: The salesperson might naturally gravitate toward recommending lower-cost solutions, thinking they are doing the client a favor, without fully exploring the client's needs and preferences for higher quality or more feature-rich products.

As my company was growing, it became obvious we needed to capitalize on raising our average tickets by offering additional services to our clients while we were already working in their homes. We sat down as a company and explained to everyone why this was important to all of us. We made sure everyone understood we would only engage in honest, ethical, and no-pressure sales in the home. Our job was to inspect the home and offer needed solutions to the client. In return, the technicians would receive a 20 percent commission on all items that were added to the job at the time of service. In our industry, this was double the common commission percentage. We wanted to share the wealth with our people too.

To do this, we needed to get our technicians to think in abundance, not scarcity. This required us to have conversations about money as a group. To talk about the amount of money many of our clients made, and how offering additional services not only would not break their banks but would also be appreciated by them because they would value preventative maintenance and life cycle expense more than any initial cost sensitivity. This type of training was crucial for our success in sales. Most of my team came from humble upbringings where money was often hard to come by. They had a hard time wrapping their heads around how my client base could spend thousands of dollars without as much as raising an eyebrow. The problem was, they did not think like my clients, and I had to teach them how to do this.

I remember having my #1 technician, who was universally loved by my clients, struggle with in-home sales. He was trusted implicitly by them; he was kind, had great communication skills, and his technical knowledge was off the charts. My only issue was he never had sold one add-on the entire time that he had worked for us. This was mind-boggling to me as my clients knew, liked, and trusted him. If anyone on my team should have been selling, it was him. One night, at an industry trade show, I called my tech at midnight to meet me at the hotel bar. I had to get to the bottom of why a guy so smart and charismatic could not sell a single service.

He was a little perplexed and I am sure annoyed as to why I got him out of bed to meet him, but he agreed to meet. As we chatted, he finally came clean with the reason he never sold: he was afraid of having more money! He then went on to tell me about his childhood and how every time his parents would get some extra money they would blow it on something stupid, causing him pain. He said it affected him so much as a kid, he decided it was just easier to not have any money beyond what was necessary to live. He felt it was just too painful to have any extra money. I was both shocked and dismayed.

So, I began the process of reframing his ideas about money and how he was not his parents. He had a solid support system at the company to help him (in fact, we got him a financial planner by trading out some carpet cleaning for time with him and his wife). I spent time helping him understand that by not offering our clients all available options, he was, in fact, choosing for them and that was not fair to our clients.

After a few weeks of this, he started to come around. All of a sudden, I would look at his numbers for the day and see a $450 add-on. The next day, $675. After that, $900 to $1000 was not uncommon. He was killing it! You see, he always had it in him to offer honest services that would help our clients. He just needed to get his mind right about money before he was able to do it.

Role-Playing

The most unpopular thing I ever did in my service business was make my team role-play. We role-played service scenarios, such as how to approach the home. We role-played sales, how to answer the phone, and where to park the vans. We made sure everyone in the company knew how to perform service and sales with a high degree of training.

Did I mention role-playing was unpopular? My team hated it. Who can really blame them, right? Getting up in front of all of your peers and performing is nerve-wracking. However, my mentor, Howard Partridge taught me the concept of business being a theater. You know what actors do in theater productions? They have rehearsals where they practice their lines and skills without the audience there. That is what we did. We rehearsed, whether the team loved it or not.

The benefit of practicing in front of your own team is you can get input from others who do the same job. You can practice using scripts to streamline the client experience. This allows you to get everyone doing and saying the same things, and you can see who on the team needs extra help and training.

Skin In the Game

Last, we must talk about rewarding those who bring in revenue for the company. Although money is not the top metric for people liking where they work, to get people to want to go the extra mile and sell your products or services, they will need some skin in the game. By coming up with a performance-based pay structure, you will incentivize your people to step out of their comfort zone and ask for the sale. You will give them the opportunity to give themselves a raise each and every day through the hard work they do to bring more revenue to the company. I am not talking about creating a boiler room, hard-core sales culture based on sleazy sales tactics and holding clients hostage in their homes with hard sales pitches. I am talking about creating a sales culture within your organization that emphasizes honest and ethical sales that will benefit the client, the company, and the salesperson. A division of revenue that can change your employee's life and yours, too.

RECAP AND ACTION ITEMS

In this chapter, I discussed how crucial it is to bridge the gap between effective marketing and making actual sales in a home services business—a lesson I learned the hard way. When I started, I was a novice in sales, wary of becoming the stereotypical "slick salesman. " But soon enough, the stark reality hit me—I needed to sell, and sell well, to support my family. I turned to every resource I could—YouTube, CDs for role-playing during drives—anything that could mold me into a better salesperson. Gradually, what started as a necessity became my passion; I learned that selling wasn't about pushing customers but about adding real value to their lives.

I also shared insights into the structured sales approach we adopted, heavily influenced by Howard Partridge's 7-Step Sales Process. This framework was a game changer, fundamentally shifting our company's approach to sales and significantly boosting our financial growth. Furthermore, I talked about the nitty-gritty of building a sales-savvy team—through constant role-playing, setting up systems of public accountability, and creating detailed sales materials to aid our techs in the field. It wasn't just about selling. It was about overcoming mental blocks related to money that held us back. We tackled these mental blocks head-on, shifting our team's mindset to one of abundance and possibility, which was essential for our growth. And let's not forget the power of incentives; by aligning rewards with performance, we motivated our team to reach new heights.

ACTION ITEMS:

- **Embrace and Refine Your Sales Skills:** No matter your personal take on sales, mastering this skill is critical. Dedicate time to learning and practicing robust sales techniques, like the 7-Step Sales Process. It's about more than just making deals; it's about genuinely serving your customers.

- **Incorporate Regular Role-Playing and Accountability:** Keep your team sharp and ready through regular role-playing sessions. These simulations prepare them for real-life scenarios, enhancing their confidence and competence. Public accountability, like showcasing sales stats, keeps everyone motivated and striving for excellence.

- **Cultivate a Positive Money Mindset in Your Team:** Tackle any limiting beliefs about money that might stifle your team's potential. Foster an environment that views money as a tool for growth and opportunity. Implementing a performance-based pay structure not only motivates but also rewards your team, making them stakeholders in the business's success.

SECTION 3:
DIGITAL MARKETING
BY KATIE HARRIS

IT'S NO SECRET THAT CONSUMERS TODAY ARE DEMANDING, YOU NEED TO BE THERE, BE VALUABLE, AND BE QUICK IN THE EXACT MOMENTS WHEN THEY ARE LOOKING FOR YOU ONLINE.

CHAPTER 8:
YOUR ONLINE PRESENCE

Eric and I have been good friends for over a decade. I remember the first time we talked like it was yesterday. We were on a video call and my digital marketing company was still in its infancy. We were onboarding his restoration company. He didn't know me and he had big goals and needed experts to help reach those goals. Eric and Larry had been working long, hard hours doing everything from operations to team building, from finance to sales, marketing, and the list goes on and on and on. Sounds familiar?

I probably sounded too enthusiastic for his liking when we first started talking about all the ways Spot On Solutions was going to help with his marketing. He stopped me. He paused a long minute and took a deep breath and said, "Listen, I'm busy," (a.k.a. don't waste my time). He continued, "I wear a lot of hats around here and I just need you to handle this." Direct and to the point. I soon learned that like most determined entrepreneurs, he did indeed wear a lot of hats and he wore them well . . . until he didn't! Over the years, he had invested in learning and marketing was one of them, but as all successful entrepreneurs do, he realized that his time could be spent better in other places, so he trusted us to handle his marketing.

An important part of an entrepreneur's journey is to know when to learn, when to do, and when to let go. All parts of the process come with growing pains and fear, but all are critical to scaling your growth. It was obvious from that first conversation that it was time for Eric to "let go" of some things he wasn't great at and make time and room for things in which he excelled. This was one hat and it was time to pass over to someone else.

As you are working to scale your business and put all the pieces together, remember to check yourself occasionally and evaluate the hats you are wearing. Ask yourself, "Is it time for me to learn, or to do, or to let go?"

I've been working directly with companies to grow their online presence since 2012. I own and operate two digital marketing agencies. Spot On Solutions specializes in the home services industry and it has put me on the front lines of marketing for hundreds of home service companies. Get Found First is a Google-managed agency and we have been trained directly at Google offices in San Francisco, Manhattan, and Chicago. We work with clients all around the world and have made the Inc.5000 list for three consecutive years. We're regularly voted a Top 10 place to work in Idaho.

I have trained owners one-on-one as well as in large groups and I'm going to share some of the most frequently asked questions and my expertise in fundamental digital marketing. Whether you are in a "learn", "a do," or a "let go" phase, there are takeaways for you in this chapter.

THE DIGITAL MARKETING PIECE

What's most important? Where do I start? Those are easily the two most common questions I get asked. When you look at all the things that you "should" be doing with digital marketing, it is easy to become totally overwhelmed. Every class you sit in, every person you talk to is going to tell you what you "should" be doing with your digital marketing and I guarantee you the minute you start to feel like you are getting a handle on it, an algorithm will change. Some of the things you need to know are foundational to the success of your digital marketing as a whole. We'll start there. Let's start with the first few things to focus on as you build a stellar foundation for your online presence.

Take a look at all of the marketing opportunities. No wonder it feels overwhelming and you don't know where to start! In this chapter, we are going to walk you through the different opportunities and help you to elevate your thinking.

DIGITAL MARKETING

You can see that the marketing strategies and tactics that you invest time and resources into point right back to your website. Your website is really the conversion point. Your marketing activities are intended to bring a strong return on investment (ROI). Those marketing activities will be designed to reach and capture your ideal clients and get them to your website so you can capture them.

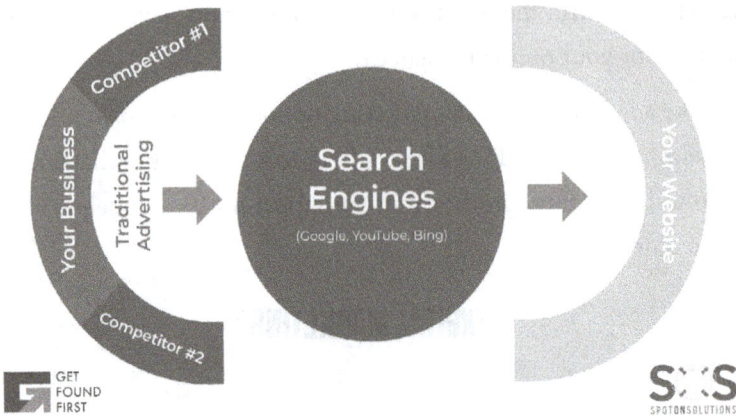

Reach Capture Convert

Always know where you are in the process.

1. ***I am doing.*** I am in a phase where I'm still wearing this hat. I am in the trenches. I am the marketing department and successful implementation is up to me.

2. ***I am learning.*** I am going to have to personally do it either because I can't afford to hire someone or I want to. I need to understand it well enough to monitor performance when someone else is managing my marketing and I want to feel secure enough to know the right questions to ask.

3. ***I am letting go!*** I am at a place where I can hire this out either internally or to an agency. I need to know how to confidently give up control. I need to have a plan to step out of the day-to-day while still effectively communicating business goals and monitoring results.

You are also going to think smarter with goals and expectations by asking if this is a *Reach, Capture, or Convert* strategy. We will help identify these as we go through all the marketing strategies calling your name.

BUILD YOUR FOUNDATION
CRAFTING A WEBSITE THAT CONVERTS FOR HOME SERVICE ENTREPRENEURS

Measure twice, cut once. Doing it right is better than doing it fast. You reap what you sow. Don't cut corners. All good advice, that I admit I heard from my parents more than once while growing up. Your website is the foundation of your marketing. You direct customers here and need it to do a lot more than just look nice.

When we first started Spot On Solutions, one of my business partners owned a restoration company. He would often tell the story of how more than once he paid someone to build him a website and "that's when all the work started for him." He learned the value of having industry experts and technical experts because your website MUST perform for two key audiences. The most important audience is your ideal customer. That person who is going to pick up the phone and call or fill out the form and request information or schedule your service. The other most important (yes there are two most important) is Google. The bots that will crawl your website and decide how to rank your content need your website to be structured correctly. Here is something to consider: a website that converts is not just a digital billboard, it's actually your digital storefront. Your customers most likely don't come to your place of business, you go to them. What would change if you started treating your website like your storefront where your customers came to shop? Your website tells your brand's story and guides visitors toward becoming paying customers. Let's break down the fundamentals of creating a website that's always open for business. I love the book "Building a StoryBrand" by Donald Miller and am constantly referring back to it as a helpful roadmap. Miller teaches that your customer is always the hero of the story! You are the guide. Just randomly check home services websites and you'll see how often your competitors are getting it wrong.

What are the first few things someone sees when they visit your website—your "digital storefront"? Research shows that you have about seven seconds to capture their attention. It's no secret that consumers today are demanding, you need to be there, be valuable, and be quick in the exact moments when they are looking for you online.

10 TIPS TO CREATE A WEBSITE THAT CONVERTS

1. Clarify Your Message

Donald Miller emphasizes the power of clear, compelling messaging in "Building a StoryBrand." Your website should immediately communicate who you are, what you offer, and how it benefits the visitor.

Craft a headline message that addresses your potential customers' needs or problems directly and remember it's not about you, they are the hero!

Follow it with a straightforward solution or promise, a benefit, and make it clear why they should choose your service over the competition. This is what sets you apart and makes you the "guide" they should choose.

2. Above the Fold . . . or Scroll Matters

I started my career as a journalist and I loved working in a bustling newsroom. We spent a lot of time every single day deciding what information should go above the fold because we knew what showed above the fold was what sold the newspapers.

Imagine you're walking past a newsstand where newspapers are displayed with only the top half visible, folded in such a way that you can only see the headlines and some key images. This top half, visible at first glance, is what entices you to pick up and read more. In the digital world, "above the fold" refers to the part of a website you see on your screen without having to scroll down.

Think of it as the first impression your website makes. Just like a catchy headline or an eye-catching photo in a newspaper is used to grab your attention, the content above the fold on your website should be so compelling that it makes visitors want to stay. It's the prime real estate of your website, where you showcase your most important message, your best deals, or the most captivating images—essentially, anything that immediately answers the "Why should I stay here?" or "How are you going to make my life better?"—for your visitors belongs in this spot.

So, in a way, treating your website's above-the-fold area like the front page of a newspaper not only grabs attention but also sets the stage for everything else that follows.

3. Visibility of Contact Information

It sounds too simple even to mention, but if you want them to call you, make sure your phone number is prominently displayed at the top of every page. Additionally, we've literally tested thousands of websites and seen that when you tell someone exactly what to do they are very likely to do it. Direct them what to do with that number with phrases like "Call Today! Call Now! Don't Wait, Available 24/7, etc." This very top section of your website is the header. To ensure your phone number is always in sight, even as potential customers scroll down your website, we use a technique called making your header sticky. This means your header, including the phone number, will "stick" to the top of the screen, remaining visible and accessible no matter how far down the page you scroll. It's like having a helpful assistant who follows you around, ready to offer assistance at any moment.

Don't forget to include a "Contact Us" link in your main navigation menu and footer. We always want it to be easy for them to know how to contact you.

4. Strategic Calls-to-Action (CTAs)

Calls-to-action (CTAs) are the signposts that guide users toward conversion, whether that's for booking a service call, requesting for a quote, or asking for a callback. Place CTAs both above the fold (visible without scrolling) and at strategic points throughout your website.

Use action-oriented language like "Get a Free Quote" or "Schedule a Service Call Today" or "Request an Inspection." If you are in the emergency service business, don't forget to add your "Available 24/7," "Call Anytime, Day or Night."

5. Emotionally Appealing Photos and Videos

As home service professionals, you have the opportunity to showcase amazing photos and videos about things that matter most to people. Their homes, their families, their pets, their safety and security. However, all too often, the first thing you see on websites is equipment or company vehicles. I know you are proud of that equipment, it speaks of how qualified you are and the quality of service you can be trusted to provide. But, remember, you are not the hero! That is not what those images say to a 36-year-old mother of three standing in a flooded basement.

Use photos and videos to reassure, bring comfort, show what life could look like if they choose to work with you. You want to use high-quality photos/videos of your team in action, showing the human side of your business. Before and after shots can be particularly persuasive, showcasing the tangible results of your services and a portfolio page along with testimonials are powerfully persuasive, especially if you can get customers to share their story in a video where they can hear the emotion in their voices and see the gratitude on their faces. Incorporating customer testimonials in video format to build trust and credibility makes the best emotionally appealing content because it is so genuine.

Do the photos and video need to be of professional quality? Honestly, this is probably what holds businesses back most often. Don't let it. Not all of your photo/video content needs to be professional or expensive. Video that is genuine can be just as impactful even if it's shot using your cell phone. Don't let a lack of professional videos/images stop you, but DO make a plan to incorporate some professional quality video into your marketing over time. The combination is a powerful conversion tool for your website.

6. Optimized for Search Engines and Users

Your website's structure should cater to both of your most important audiences which are: the humans you want as customers; and the search engines where you want to rank. It should be easy to navigate and rank well on relevant queries.

You want to research and integrate relevant keywords naturally into your content, titles, and meta descriptions. These keywords will include your services, business name, service locations, etc. Structuring your pages correctly helps Google and other search engines know how to index and rank your content.

With a large number of searches happening on mobile, ensure your site is responsive and loads quickly on all devices. According to Statista, a reputable provider of market and consumer data, "in 2023 almost 50 percent of web traffic in the United States originated from mobile devices ." This statistic is low for emergency home service companies where you can expect the majority of people to turn to their mobile device in their moment of need.

Finally, keep your navigation simple so your visitors and the search engines can find what they are looking for quickly. Your menu needs to be simple and intuitive.

7. Showcasing Trust Signals

Build trust by showcasing your credentials, awards, and affiliations promi-nently. These don't have to be above the fold, but can be depending on your customer. You do want to make sure they are somewhere on your web-site, including internal pages. Further down your homepage and on your internal pages—this is where you want to display badges for your industry certifications or memberships in professional associations.

The ultimate trust signal is your reviews! We're going to spend a whole section talking about them. Consider putting your reviews above the scroll. Customer reviews are powerful trust signals.

8. Domain Authority and Content Strategy

Domain Authority (DA) is a search engine ranking score that predicts how likely a website is to rank on search engine result pages (SERPs). Increasing your Domain Authority involves creating valuable content and earning backlinks from reputable sites. In September 2023, Google rolled out its "Helpful Content Update" making this more important than ever.

A hot topic right now is, "Can you use AI (Artificial Intelligence), things like ChatGPT to create your content for you?" In a Search Engine Land article, they quote Danny Sullivan, Google's Search Liaison, where he reiterated some of what was said, previously, about Google's stance on this topic.

Sullivan wrote on Twitter on the topic of AI-generated content, "Content created primarily for search engine rankings, however, it is done, is against our guidance." But he added that, "If content is helpful & created for people first, that's not an issue."[2] [3]

---

2 https://searchengineland.com/google-search-on-using-ai-to-write-content-391728

3 https://developers.google.com/search/docs/fundamentals/creating-helpful-content
https://searchengineland.com/library/platforms/google/google-algorithm-updates/helpful-content-update

Sullivan references the revised E-E-A-T quality raters guidelines, saying, "For anyone who uses *any method* to generate a lot of content primarily for search rankings, our core systems look at many signals to reward content clearly demonstrating E-E-A-T (experience, expertise, authoritativeness, and trustworthiness)."

So, you can use AI to generate content. You can definitely use it to help you get started, but be sure to put your human touch to it and remain focused on your customer.

Now that we know exactly how important "helpful content" is to Google, it seems obvious that every website needs a blog function added. A blog is the best way to consistently add current and relevant content that meets the "helpful content" rules. Start a blog to share your expertise, answer common customer questions, offer solutions, and showcase your company, all of which can improve your search engine rankings and attract more visitors. **Bonus Tip:** *Don't forget the emotional photos and videos that you can add to your blog content.*

9. Analyzing and Adapting

Your website really isn't complete until you have installed analytics to track your site's performance, understand visitor behavior, and identify areas for improvement.

According to Google, starting July 1, 2023, standard Universal Analytics properties stopped processing new data, and all customers will lose access to the Universal Analytics interface and API effective July 1, 2024. By the time this is published, Google Analytics 4 (GA4) is the analytics tool you should have installed on your website.[4]

The ability to monitor metrics such as page views, bounce rate, and conversion rate to gauge your website's effectiveness is an invaluable tool to understand your ideal customer and their behavior. The better you get at

---

4 https://support.google.com/analytics/answer/11583528?hl=en#:~:text=Starting%20 on%20July%201%2C%202023,starting%20on%20July%201%2C%202024.

understanding the data, the better you can optimize marketing strategies to grow your business. One of the biggest advantages of digital marketing is the opportunity to make data-driven decisions.

10. Regular Updates and Maintenance

A great website is never truly finished. Regular updates and maintenance are crucial for keeping your content fresh, your technology up to date, and your site's security tight. Regularly review and update the services you offer, testimonials, and your portfolio page. The most overlooked updates are adding new before and after photos (emphasis on the after), updating testimonials, and refreshing images on the homepage.

Keep your software and plug-ins updated to protect against security vulnerabilities. Outdated plug-ins are often to blame for website issues.

Finally, be willing to make changes based on data, whether it's tweaking your CTAs, adjusting your messaging, or redesigning your navigation. Don't let your website be a build-it-and-forget-it project. It is the conversion piece of your marketing. It is your digital storefront. Treat it as such!

BONUS TIP: Showcase your reviews on your website. We could really emphasize the importance of reviews on your website here, but it will be a whole section talking about the value of reviews in your marketing as a whole, for now, remember to include your reviews on your website.

WEBSITE WRAP-UP

Remember, a website that converts is not just about looking good—it's about being strategic, intentional, and user-focused at every turn. I really love how Miller teaches us about focusing on the customer. He says, "If you confuse, you'll lose. Be clear, and your customers will listen."

Focus on your user and everything else will follow. As I've learned from Miller's lessons, one of my favorite takeaways is that "when we talk about our businesses, we are usually talking about *our* solutions. This is a mistake. Customers aren't looking for solutions.

They are looking for somebody who understands *their* problems." LIVE customer-focused! Frame your messaging and website content around your customer's needs and challenges rather than just the services or products offered. With your foundation firmly in place, you can confidently drive your marketing efforts to your website that converts!

DON'T FORGET...TODAY'S
CONSUMER IS SMART!
THEY ARE GOING TO
LOOK AND SEE WHEN THE
REVIEW WAS AND IF IT WAS
OVER SIX MONTHS AGO,
IT LOSES SOME IMPACT.

CHAPTER 9:
GOOGLE BUSINESS PROFILE

Every business needs a Google Business Profile (GBP)—you might have known it better as Google My Business (GMB) before it was rebranded in 2021. Over the years, Google has shown a real commitment to this platform, but it has gone through several name changes. Some of these changes felt like a full-blown identity crisis. What started as Google Local and Google Places, became Google+ Local, then Google My Business, but Google seems to have really settled in the Google Business Profile and we're seeing it evolve into a comprehensive, fairly user-friendly tool. It is tied to some vital resources for businesses, including navigation, customer reviews, helpful content updates, and most recently Local Service Ads also known as Google Guaranteed.

While the name or branding behind this platform has changed, the intent behind it has remained pretty consistent.

- **Enhanced Visibility:** Help your business show up on Google Search and Maps and make it easier for customers to find your service.

- **Centralize Information Management:** Help customers find your name, address, phone number, and services offered. It's important that your name, address, and phone number (NAP) stay consistent across Google. It's recommended that you make your GBP the master for that information and make everything else consistent with it.

- **Customer Interaction:** Reviews! Reviews! Reviews! This lets your customers engage with your business online and builds trust and credibility. Customers can also ask questions on your profile.

- **Analytics:** This is another opportunity to make data-driven decisions based on your customer interactions. Who is finding you and how are they interacting with your business? There are answers in the GBP analytics.

OPTIMIZING GBP FOR YOUR HOME SERVICE BUSINESS

Once you understand the intent and platform, you can begin making optimizations to show up higher and own more internet real estate space. Consider where Google Business Profiles show up on the Search Engine Results Page (SERP). It stands out and the click is free, unlike the paid options above it. It's pretty prime real estate!

Set-Up the Basics

Your name, address, and phone number (NAP) should be accurate here and should be the master for all other online listings, including all directories. Once your profile is verified with Google, you can change your physical address to a service area. At the time of publishing, you choose a primary category that describes your business as a whole, be as specific as possible. You must choose a category from the dropdown menu provided. If the category isn't available, choose a more general category that accurately describes your business. You cannot create your own category. You can get the most up-to-date information directly from Google.[5]

This is critically important for home service businesses where you are reliant on servicing an area, rather than people coming to your place of business. In addition to submitting your NAP, you are going to add your website URL and check back occasionally to make sure your basic information is accurate.

Get Reviews! Reply to Reviews!

Did you know that customers trust reviews on Google as much as they trust someone they know personally? There are so many studies out there and they all agree reviews significantly impact the perception of your business and customer choices. What do you think is more important—to have a lot of reviews or have current reviews? It's really a trick question because both have something you want.

But, Google is clear. They want to see you with a consistent flow of reviews. It really is better to have some reviews rolling in every week rather than hundreds of reviews hitting all at once and then no more coming. That signals something fraudulent and even good reviews can get throttled. On the other hand, customers do look and see who has the most reviews, and sometimes "the most" wins! If I need a carpet cleaner in my area and one has 16 reviews and the other one has 580, I automatically assume the one with the most reviews is better.

Don't forget . . . today's consumer is smart! They are going to look and see when the last review was and if it was over six months ago, it loses some impact. A BrightLocal survey found that 73 percent of consumers only pay attention to reviews written in the last month. If you can show a steady increase in reviews, the recent reviews will resonate and give you an edge.

---

5 https://support.google.com/business/answer/3480441?hl=en

Do you need to have all 5-star reviews? No, you don't. Especially if you have a lot of reviews. We expect that some people are just going to complain. Some research shows that a perfect 5-star rating can be a red flag. If you are in the 4.6 stars and better, then you hold a powerfully persuasive position. At least quarterly, you should evaluate your reviews and how they stack up with your competition. You should have a goal of consistently adding new reviews. You should know who is winning the review race in your market. You should have a plan to be that winner! If you are a new company, this may take some time, but chances are your commitment to consistency will yield ranking rewards.

What about replying to reviews? The answer is simple. Yes . . . Always! Of course, you need to reply to negative reviews to combat any negative impressions. Businesses tend to be pretty good at this, mostly because we usually have a side of the story we'd like to tell. We'll talk more about this in the Search Engine Optimization (SEO) section. Replying to all reviews can help with your organic rankings.

Do you reply to your positive reviews? I certainly hope so! Think about it, if someone took time out of their day to walk up to you and personally give you a compliment——what would you do? You would stop what you were doing and you would genuinely say, "Thank you!" Yet, oftentimes when someone does just that online, we essentially turn our backs and walk away. How rude!

That same BrightLocal study found that 20 percent of consumers expect to receive a response to their review within one day. Furthermore, 89 percent of consumers read businesses' responses to reviews, indicating that the way a business engages with reviews can affect its reputation and consumer perception.

Make it a rule, create a system, train your team—from this point on you reply to all reviews.

Add Photos and Videos

Typically, Google Business Profiles have a photo of the exterior of the building. For service businesses, this may not be as relevant, and once a profile is verified, you may want to change this to a team picture in front of your trucks or something more appropriate for how your customers engage with you. But, that's just the beginning. You should be adding photos and videos regularly to your profile.

This can be a very strategic way to earn rankings for a variety of areas you service. This is also a great opportunity to showcase your team in action with customers and/or serving in the community where you can show hyper-local photos and videos.

Just like we discussed with the emotional appeal of photos and videos for your website, the same applies to your profile. Show your team. Showcase your work. With customers' permission, post from a job site and use geo-tagging to signal Google to indicate your service area.

Add Updates

Google loves current and relevant content and the updates tab in GBP is meant for that! It feels a lot like a mix of a blog post and a social media update. It's a great way to multi-use content from either your website or your social media and turn it into a GBP update. Definitely shorter than a blog post, but a little more than a social post—it's a nice mix designed to provide "helpful content" to users searching on Google. It's simple to add images to your posts, so if you have the perfect picture that you'd like to post, just create a few paragraphs of content to go with it. Be sure to include keywords that you want to rank on and you have a GBP update. Here are some ideas to get you started with GBP updates:

Highlight Your Services

Showcase Special Offers: Regularly post about any special offers, discounts, or promotions you're running. When you post offer updates you are able to set expiration dates.

Highlight Services: Periodically spotlight different services you offer, especially those that may be relevant to the upcoming season.

Before and After Photos

Quality of Work: Share before and after photos of your projects. This visual evidence of your service can significantly boost trust and interest among potential customers, especially when combined with a testimonial.

Share Customer Reviews and Testimonials

Leverage Positive Feedback: Whenever you receive a glowing review, create a post thanking the customer and sharing their feedback. This not only shows appreciation but also serves as social proof to prospective clients.

Video Testimonials: If possible, share video testimonials. They are highly engaging and can convey customer satisfaction more effectively than text.

Offer Helpful Tips

Educate Your Audience: Share useful tips related to your services. You can really hit the helpful content mark with "tips" and "how to" updates. You also provide value to your potential customers. This positions your business as an expert in your field and can help build trust with your audience.

Highlights About Your Team/Business

Pull Back the Curtain: Let people meet your people. Shout them out. Show what happens when no one is looking. Share your company values and how your team is living them. It will make you real and likable.

Timely Updates: Share updates related to changes in service hours, availability during holidays, or any special weather events.

Utilize Events and Mini-Blogs

Event Announcements: If you're participating in or hosting any local events, make sure to post about them. Consider sharing any local Chamber of Commerce events, CE classes, Lunch and Learns you might be hosting.

If your team is off-site at an industry event getting training, that makes great content as well.

Mini-Blogs: Share short updates or stories about your business, such as community involvement or milestones. This humanizes your brand and builds a connection with your audience.

Optimize for SEO

Incorporate Keywords: Naturally include relevant keywords in your updates to improve your visibility in search results related to your services. You should find focus keywords scattered throughout your profile, but it can be strategically planned with your updates.

Add Q&As

We assume that we need to wait for customers to leave a question for us on our profile, but in reality, this is one of the best-kept secrets hidden away in your profile to help you rank for free. If Google's intent is to have helpful content for users, then give it to them! You know the questions that are most frequently asked, so ask them on your profile and then answer them!

You can proactively post questions and answers using keywords that will both serve to provide valuable information to your customer and also feed the search engines with quality content you can rank for.

If you have a FAQs section on your website, start there! Take those questions and post them to your profile. Carefully state the questions in a way that sounds normal and natural and appealing to your customer. Then strategically post answers that have keywords and high-value content.

After you get your most frequently asked questions posted, consider adding common misconceptions where you can provide helpful information to your potential customers.

What do all of these have in common? They are free for you. The name may change again, the platform will most definitely evolve, but stay focused on the intent of the user and your profile will rank.

GOOGLE BUSINESS PROFILE WRAP-UP

The home service industry is competitive. Use Google Business Profile to increase visibility, engage with your audience, and grow your business. Remember the goal is to provide value to your potential customers and improve your online presence while doing it so you can be the go-to source in your market.

Consistency is going to play a key role in your success with Google Business Profile. Consistently check your information and make sure it's updated, consistently request and reply to reviews, consistently add photos, videos, and updates focusing on keywords. Increase your trust and credibility with potential customers and improve your visibility on Google.

As a challenge, I encourage you to set a goal to engage with your Google Business Profile actively over the next month. This could involve updating your business information, posting weekly updates about your services or promotions, responding to every new review, or experimenting with different types of posts to see what resonates with your audience.

MASTERING PAID ADS FOR HOME SERVICES: A GOOGLE ADS GUIDE

Remember at the beginning of this chapter we talked about how understanding digital marketing can feel overwhelming for a business owner? This is the place where it starts to feel like digital marketing is a foreign language! Add to it the fact that Google is notorious for "changing things" just when you start to figure it out and there is a little bit of the learning curve left.

One of the first questions you have to answer is, "What is your goal?" When someone comes to me and they need the phone ringing ASAP, then I tell them that ads are usually the starting place to invest your marketing dollars. It is a faster route to phone calls than an SEO strategy and the user intent is much higher than with a social media strategy. When a potential customer searches on Google (or any search engine) their INTENT is clear. User intent is most clear when THEY are actively searching for you and your service. Compare this to social media where the user (your potential customer) is just casually scrolling their newsfeed—you have no idea what their intent is. Social media marketing is much more disruptive and user intent is unknown.

I also like to compare it to renting versus buying a home. You are renting Google's space, and once you stop paying your ads disappear. They no longer show up at all. The advantage is you have specific targeting for the type of leads you are looking for which creates more incoming phone calls which is obviously a faster route to your ROI.

So . . . where do paid ads fit into your marketing strategy? Should Google Ads be part of the plan and what exactly does that really mean?

If it feels like there is a lot to know when it comes to paid ads, it's because there is. When we refer to Google Ads, we are talking about all of these types of advertising opportunities. Google Ads can be particularly effective for home services businesses, offering targeted advertising based on user search intent.

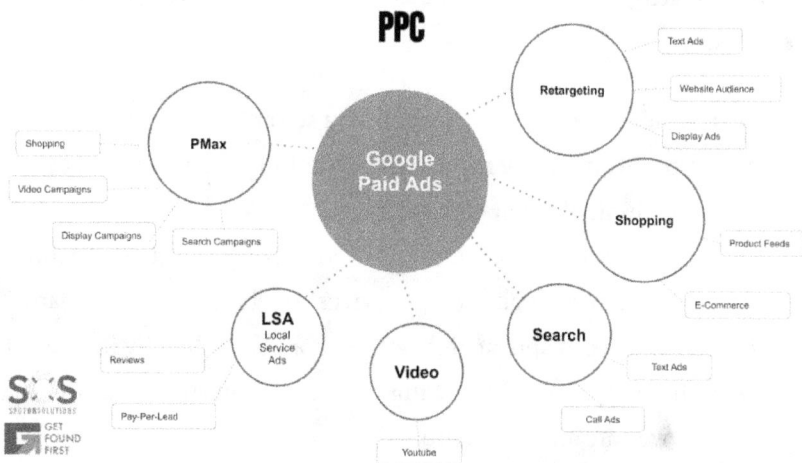

Let's dive into the world of Google Ads. Imagine you've got a billboard that only shows up to people already interested in what you offer, exactly when they are looking for you—that's Google Ads in a nutshell. It's designed to put your home services business in front of potential customers precisely when they're searching for the services you provide.

Google Ads operates on a pay-per-click (PPC) basis, meaning you pay when someone clicks on your ad. It's like fishing in a pond stocked with fish already biting! The trick is getting a cost per acquisition that yields a return on your investment.

Basically, catching the fish you want for the cost it's worth to you. Pay-Per-Click ads have historically been top of the search engine results page (SERP); for some service industries, it's now number two, just under Google's Pay-Per-Lead model called Local Service Ads, also known as Google Guaranteed.

TYPES OF GOOGLE ADS

Depending on your goals and budget, there are several types of Google Ads to choose from and implement. When someone refers to Google Ads, be sure to clarify the exact type of ads that they are referring to. Let's break them down:

- **Search Ads**: These are the text ads you see at the top of Google's search results page when you look something up. This is what you probably think of when we say PPC ads.

  For a home services business, this is gold. Because when someone types in "emergency plumbing services" or "best HVAC company," your business can appear right at the top. You're directly in line with what they're looking for, making them highly likely to click through to your website and take action.

- **Display/Remarketing Ads**: Think of display and remarketing ads as digital billboards spread across the internet. These are visual ads that appear on Google's partner websites, targeting users based on their previous online activities or demographics. For example, someone who's been researching home renovation ideas sees your ad for home improvement services as they browse related sites. It's a way to remind them, "Hey, we're here to help!"

  You've already paid for the click, sent the postcard, or done the boots-on-the-ground marketing to drive someone to your website once, if they didn't convert, you don't want to lose them. Remarketing puts your visual ad back in front of them when they are online reinforcing your message and keeping your business in front of them through a decision-making process.

- **Video Ads**: With the popularity of video content skyrocketing, video ads are your chance to engage potential customers on YouTube and other video platforms. These ads can be especially effective for home services businesses by showcasing your work, offering DIY tips to add value, and showing expertise. This is also a powerful place to share customer testimonials. It's a dynamic way to build trust and show off your expertise. In case you didn't know, Google owns YouTube, so these platforms share information giving you expanded reach to your target audience.

- **Shopping Ads**: If your business sells products related to home services, such as tools, fixtures, or cleaning products, Google Shopping ads can boost your visibility. These ads show users a photo of your product, a title, the price, and your store name right at the top of Google search. It's like having your product on the shelf right at the entrance of the largest online store. Products may also include digital or in-person courses you offer.

- **PerformanceMax or Pmax** is an ad type that leverages the power of computer learning and simplifies the ad placement process. Basically, Google decides where your ad should show up individually for customers depending on where Google deems they are most likely to convert. We are going to continue to see AI exponentially increase the speed at which the paid platforms are able to deliver results for businesses. I anticipate advertising options powered by machine learning will continue to amaze us. There are things coming that we haven't even imagined possible yet—be ready for them!

Each of these ad types offers a unique way to connect with your audience, whether they're actively searching for your services, casually browsing related topics, or watching relevant videos. The key is to match your advertising strategy with your business goals and the preferences of your target customers, or in the case of Pmax, let Google do it for you.

It's important to make sure your conversion tracking is set up correctly; it's critical with Performance Max. Good "data in" gets good "conversions out." Bad conversion data will waste your money.

In the most simplified form, Google Ads is about putting your home services business in front of the right people, at the right time. With a bit of strategy and some fine-tuning, it can be a game changer for your business, driving leads, bookings, and ultimately, revenue.

But, we all know it's not simple. Having campaigns structured correctly is imperative. Whether you are doing or learning or letting go, there is value in understanding some of the language and processes.

Technically speaking, you need to make sure your campaigns are structured correctly. This includes, but is not limited to:

- Keyword Research

- Keyword Match Types

- Creating Compelling Ads

- Ad Extensions

- Bidding Strategies

- Setting Your Budget

- Conversion Tracking

- Analyzing and Optimizing

Google Local Service Ads

Also known as "Google Guaranteed," Google Local Service Ads (LSAs) deserve their own shout-out here. At the time of this publishing, Local Service Ads have the premier placement on a Search Engine Results Page (SERP). They get the top spot! Above everything else, you'll find the paid ads with a little green checkmark proving YOU are Google Guaranteed.

So, not only do LSAs take the top spot on the page but they also get an extra boost of credibility from Google essentially saying that Google recommends you above your competition.

On top of all of that, these ads are Pay-Per-Lead rather than Pay-Per-Click. If someone clicks on and calls from your LSA but they are not an actual lead, you don't pay. This protects you from paying for solicitation calls, job seeker calls, and even "that guy" who works for you and keeps clicking on your ad to get your phone number! (Everybody has "that guy" !)

You might be wondering, "So what is the downside?"—that all sounds pretty good! The downside is that LSAs are not available for every service, although the list is quickly growing. You are limited to the categories Google has set; so, you may not be able to advertise for everything you'd like to advertise for. There is also a different dashboard, separate from the main Google Ads dashboard where LSAs are managed. This dashboard includes where you set your weekly budget (which Google will recommend to you), where you manage the leads—this includes disputing and archiving leads. It also has a separate place to request reviews specifically from your LSA customers. All of this is fairly user-friendly, but it is another hat to put on, so you'll need to decide "Should *I* do this, should I learn this, or should I let this go to someone else."

Local Service Ads are one of the marketing strategies that does NOT direct a potential customer to your website for conversion to happen! Actually, there is no option for them to click and go to your website. Google wants the conversion to happen right there, so if you are unhappy with your website and working to improve it, this may be a good option to reach and convert clients quickly.

My agencies actively manage millions of dollars of ad spending across a variety of industries and across the country, even internationally. We have found the combination of a Pay-Per-Lead and Pay-Per-Click strategy to be powerful. We find that one enhances the other and gives you multiple levers to pull in strategically, finding your ideal customer, reaching them at their moment of need, and ultimately acquiring them at a cost that makes sense for your marketing goals.

PAID ADS WRAP-UP

If both PPC and LSA ads are an option for your business, that doesn't mean you are required to do both. It does mean you have some great options to target your ideal customer when their intent on using your services is high!

The easier you make it for someone to find you in their moment of need, the more likely you are to win their business.

It's important to structure your ad campaigns currently in order to get the best results and ROI. Google will give you recommendations, but technically speaking, the structure and management of your ads campaigns are critical. You have a lot of levers to pull here and can strategically find what type of ads work best in your market.

ALWAYS TELL GOOGLE THE TRUTH AND AS MUCH OF THE TRUTH ABOUT WHO YOU ARE, WHAT YOU DO, ABOUT YOUR SERVICES, AND GOOGLE WILL REWARD YOU WITH RANKINGS.

CHAPTER 10:
SEARCH ENGINE OPTIMIZATION & SOCIAL MEDIA

When I started my agency in 2012, we primarily focused on Search Engine Optimization (SEO) and website design. When we started, the organic listings that come from good SEO were displayed at the top of the SERP. Do a Google search and the top thing that you would see is the organic listing, but the landscape has drastically changed since "the olden days" of digital marketing. Now, you find the organic listings much lower on the results page.

Today, the digital landscape looks different. As the digital landscape changed, so did our marketing company and services and you need to be willing to pivot and adjust marketing strategies based on the digital landscape and your customers.

Organic rankings are no longer at the top of the page, ranking #1 looks different than it did a decade ago. At the very top of the page, you'll find Local Service Ads, then Pay-Per-Click ads, followed by Google Business Profiles, and below that the organic listings.

What does that mean for you? Is SEO still important? Is it more important or less important than paid ads? Should I invest in both SEO and Paid Ads? Do people click on ads more than organic listings? These are some of the questions that we always get asked. Let me try to answer them for you.

SEO may be one of the hardest marketing strategies for you, the business owner who is already wearing a ton of hats, to understand "what is my agency doing" or "how do I know what to do." It can feel very black box, but at the heart of it, Search Engine Optimization is really just about telling Google (and all the other search engines) exactly what they need to know. You see, Google is Google because we know that when we search for something, we are going to find results for what we are looking for. Sometimes it feels like Google even knows me better than I know myself and there is some truth to that because of the massive machine learning that sees and records every single thing I do online.

You see, even though it feels like things are always changing with Google—the algorithms change, the ad types change, the SERP changes, etc.—one thing that never changes is that Google is always focused on the end user. Google cares deeply that when its customer searches (anyone searching for something online is its ideal customer), the person searching finds the most relevant answer for their search query. When we understand what is most important to Google, it helps us understand SEO better.

So, always tell Google the truth and as much of the truth about who you are, what you do, about your services, etc. and Google will reward you with rankings, because Google wants you to show up for people looking for exactly what you offer when they search for it.

Sounds easy enough, but how you tell Google all of that information matters. I remember when I was in elementary school and we went to the library, they taught us all about the card catalog system, the Dewey decimal system for finding books in the library. You would pull the little drawer out and inside would be all the cards organized in alphabetic order, so you could literally find anything in a massive library in a matter of minutes.

Your website is not much different. It is the card catalog system that Google needs to search to find what it's looking for so it can easily index and rank the content on your website for potential customers to find easily. The difference is that Google needs to be able to find anything that anyone searches for and deliver results from a worldwide web in milliseconds. The easier your website makes it for Google to search and index your content, the better you will rank for the variety of keywords your customers are searching for.

3 MAIN THINGS TO FOCUS ON WITH SEO

1. Domain Authority: What is domain authority? Why does it matter? Add the link to moz.com so people can check their domain authority.

2. Website Structure: Titles and descriptions

3. Keyword research: What you think you should rank for may not actually be where the search volume is. Combine what you hear customers asking with what Google says people are searching for and create great content around those things. Content is more than just the pages on your website. Content is the blog posts, content is the photos (use ALT tags), content is the videos. Embed videos and rank on YouTube. Content is reviews people leave for you and your response to them.

SEO WRAP-UP

The intent behind Search Engine Optimization hasn't changed. It's all about giving the user exactly what they are looking for. In order to do this effectively, you need a website with a strong domain authority. You need to have your website structured currently so the search engine bots can crawl your website to index your content and rank it. Because Google cares most about its customer (the person doing the search), adding current and relevant content is more valuable than ever.

Is SEO still important? YES! Definitely.

Is it more important or less important than paid ads? That depends. What are your marketing goals and what is your budget? In a perfect world, you have a holistic marketing strategy where you can own as much internet real estate space as possible, but in reality, you may just need to get the phone ringing as fast as possible, and paid ads might need to be the focus. Like owning a home, SEO is an investment. It takes more time to earn than rankings. But, once you own them they are easier to keep.

Should I invest in both SEO and Paid Ads? When your budget allows, yes! You want to own as much internet real estate space as possible. Think of it this way—if you owned every store in the mall what are the chances that I would shop at your store? Pretty high, right? The same is true of your digital storefront. The more places you show up, the higher the chances that people "shop" with you.

Do people click on ads more than organic listings? This depends . . . what do you do? Do you click on ads or scroll down to the organic listings? Everyone behaves differently and you want to capture and convert as many potential customers as you can, so the better you understand your ideal client, the better you may know this. Remember, you are not your ideal customer, so don't make the decision on what YOU do.

What we know is that when your business shows up in the paid ads and then organically, your click-through rate incrementally increases based on where you show up organically. This means, that even if someone doesn't click on your ad and scrolls down to find you, the chances they click on your organic listing increases dramatically if they also saw you in the ads.

Bottomline—invest in the house! It may take more time to see direct results, but with a smart and consistent strategy, the investment will pay off and the rankings you will own could save you money in the long run and yield ongoing results.

SOCIAL MEDIA MARKETING

If your goal is to reach more people, then social media marketing is a strategy to focus on. If your goal is to immediately get the phone ringing, social media might not be the first place to invest depending on your industry.

Remember the intent of the user matters. We simply don't know the intent of someone who engages with your post or ad on social media. Social media marketing is very disruptive. You are basically inserting your business and message into someone else's day by showing up for them. You don't know what they are doing or if they even need or want your service at that time. What you do know is that when potential customers "see" you online over and over again, they can feel like they know you . . . and even better, they can like and trust you before they even meet you or need you.

Imagine that, what if your potential customers knew your name, liked you, and trusted you before they needed you?! You are giving yourself a huge advantage when the time comes that they do need you.

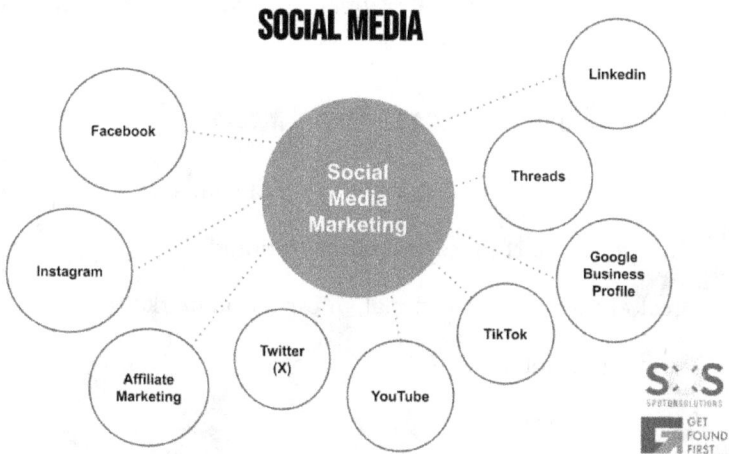

SOCIAL MEDIA

The most asked question I get about social media is where should I be? Facebook, Instagram, TikTok, LinkedIn, Twitter—the options can feel endless and overwhelming. My answer is, "Where are your customers hanging out?" That's where YOU need to be. People make the mistake of thinking they need to be everywhere. So they take the same post and put it everywhere. A much better plan is to follow your user! Hang out where your people hang out and adjust your social posts to them.

For example, your ideal customer may be a 50–65 year-old woman. Research shows she is probably still hanging out on Facebook and probably Instagram. Did you know there are about 241 million active users on Facebook? Chances are still high that your audience is there too.

Be there with posts that make you likable and add value. Be their expert in your space and willingly share your best advice to make her life better, safer, smarter. This same ideal customer might also be on LinkedIn, so be there as well. But, on LinkedIn, you may need to show up a little differently. Here you can be a thought leader and set yourself apart from the crowd. Be smart. Be professional. Add value everywhere you hang out online.

What Is The Purpose of Being On Social Media?

- Engage with your audience at the top of your sales funnel
- Help people start to "care about your brand"
- Break through the traditional, interruption marketing
- Create "promoters"
- Trigger Impulses

The Types of Content on Social Media

It's about more than just a post. The types of content you create connect differently. Not only do you need to figure out who your audience is, but you need to know what they care about so you know the best types of content to provide. This allows them to know, like, and trust you. Here are some types of posts from the most basic to the more engaging types. What does your audience like?

- Text posts
- Images
- Videos
- Stories
- Reels
- Live Posts

Know your Brand Voice

What is your brand's voice? It's easy when you, as the owner, are the one handling your social media but what happens when it's time to let go of this hat and give it to someone else?

Clearly understanding your brand's voice is important so that no matter who is posting for your company, the brand that people know, like, and trust stays true.

I highly recommend you do a brainstorming session to identify your brand's voice. You can do this alone, but if you have a team, I strongly encourage you to include them and hear what they think your brand's voice is. Brands have a personality of their own. It's this personality that attracts the right customers. Is your brand personality-friendly, professional, silly, educational— what words describe your brand?

ACTIVITY: Spend 5–10 minutes and brainstorm every word that describes your brand voice. Encourage people to say the first things that come to their mind. Write them on a big Post-it paper or whiteboard, but get them up in front of everyone.

Once all the words are up, let everyone vote for the top three. The one they think best describes your brand voice gets three votes, the second choice gets two votes, and the third gets one vote.

After everyone has voted, it's time for the owner/owners to vote. Be sure to let others go first so the owner doesn't sway their true votes by showing his/hers first.

Now, tally your votes. Identify the top 3–5 words that embody your business and discuss them. Do these ring true? Is this the brand voice/personality that you want to shine through when anyone posts for your company? Did you keep the user in mind?

Congrats! Once you've identified these words, you can stay on brand every time you or your team posts and engages on social media.

SOCIAL MEDIA WRAP-UP

Social media is a disruptive marketing strategy. We interrupt people with social media and don't know their intent when they engage with us. They might think your post was just funny or they might be considering your services—you just don't know.

What you do know is that once you truly understand your brand voice and have identified your ideal client, you can reach them through social media in a way that makes them know, like, and trust you before they even need you. Social media is a massive reach tool for your marketing and it can even be a place to convert customers. Know your audience, know where they are, and then consistently show up there, armed with value.

Digital marketing can mean a lot of different things and getting clear on your marketing goals can help simplify where you want to focus your marketing efforts.

Start by getting clear on who your ideal customer is. Remember to focus on the user in all that you do. Know what matters to them and be where they are.

Make sure your foundation is strong. Do you have a website that converts for both of the most important audiences? You have two main audiences to consider—your ideal customer and the search engine bots who will be crawling and indexing your site.

As your business grows, so will you and your team. This means the time will come when you can start taking off some of the hats you wear. Are you doing, learning, or letting go of the marketing strategies? There is a time for all of these things, but as your business grows more and more, you should consider letting go so you can focus on things that only you can do and the things you do best.

RECAP AND ACTION ITEMS FOR SECTION 3

In this section, I shared a pivotal moment in my career in digital marketing, focusing on a significant partnership with my client, Eric. At the start, Eric was overwhelmed with the multitude of tasks required to run his company, from operations to marketing. He soon realized the importance of focusing on what he excelled at and made the strategic decision to delegate his marketing needs to my company, Spot On Solutions, which specializes in digital marketing for the home services industry.

This story highlights an essential skill for entrepreneurs: knowing when to learn something new, when to take charge, and when to delegate. This ability is crucial for scaling a business effectively and optimizing operational efficiency. Using Eric's example, I underline the importance of relinquishing tasks where one may lack expertise, thereby allowing more room to concentrate on one's strengths and core business areas.

Moreover, I discuss my extensive experience in digital marketing, detailing the evolution of my companies and our notable achievements. The chapter offers practical advice on crafting effective digital marketing strategies, prioritizing tasks, and making strategic decisions in business management.

ACTION ITEMS:

- **Evaluate My Role:** I will regularly assess the tasks I am handling in my business to identify where I might be better off delegating to enhance efficiency and focus on my strengths.

- **Embrace Learning:** I will allocate time to learning new skills essential for my business but also recognize when it is more cost-effective to hire expertise instead of continuing the learning curve.

- **Focus on Core Competencies:** I will pinpoint the areas where I excel and ensure that I am directing most of my energy and resources toward these parts of my business to maximize growth and profitability.

- **Let Go When Necessary:** I need to be ready to hand over responsibilities when it becomes clear that other individuals or teams can handle them better, as this can lead to better performance and growth.

- **Regularly Review Marketing Strategies:** I will keep myself updated on the latest trends in digital marketing and regularly evaluate my marketing strategies to ensure they align with the best practices and effectively target my audience.

These steps are crafted to help entrepreneurs and business owners like me optimize our roles, focus on growth, and manage our marketing strategies more effectively for better returns.

SECTION 4:
BUILDING A HIGH-PERFORMANCE TEAM

I NEEDED TO CREATE A COMPANY CULTURE WHERE PEOPLE WANTED TO COME TO WORK. A COMPANY WHERE TALENTED PEOPLE WANTED TO DEVOTE THEMSELVES TO A HIGHER PURPOSE THAN JUST MY AMBITION AND EGO.

CHAPTER 11:

GREAT CULTURE IS THE FOUNDATION OF YOUR SCALABLE COMPANY

The word culture drives so many people crazy. What does a good one look like? How do I know if mine is bad? Does "culture" even matter? It is such an esoteric idea for so many people, especially hard-charging business owners who want to grind and run the business strictly by the numbers (or in many cases by their bank account) and don't feel culture is important for them or their employees.

I have to admit, I used to be one of those owners myself. I didn't feel it was my responsibility to make sure everyone was happy. Not my place to make sure people feel fulfilled. Certainly not my problem with what my people had going on outside of work. I just felt as if it was an equation. I market to get work, you do the work I get for you, and I pay you every Friday. Simple!

Except life does not work that way and that thinking created a disaster of a company for me. I did not use the lessons I had learned many years before while playing sports in school; that team chemistry and a feeling of being part of something bigger than oneself often would triumph over more skilled teams. I was on some teams in my youth where we were like the movie "The Bad News Bears." On the outside, we looked like a mess, but we got along well and made sure we tried hard for each other so we could win. We took down opponents who looked far better than us on paper because our team spirit and gritty nature outplayed the star-studded teams who lacked good chemistry. We had a culture of winning, and that's what we did.

I learned the hard way our company needed the same culture as my childhood teams. For us to win as a team, we needed good chemistry and team culture. I played on many teams in my youth that looked like real winners on paper. However, those teams rarely won because all the star athletes were more concerned with their individual accolades and glory than being good team players. The winningest teams I played on in my youth were selfless. The players had each other's backs and were willing to sacrifice personal achievement in order for the team to win. These teams had chemistry, caring for each other, and a team culture. This was what won ballgames, not one person being the superstar and everybody else working for him to succeed.

Yet, that was how I was acting within my own company. I was the superstar and I treated everyone else in the company as just a role player; there to assist me. I looked at every action we took and every person in the company as just a disposable piece of this big puzzle. I was dehumanizing people to meet the end I desired. I never set out to dehumanize anyone, but I am, by my nature, a very task-oriented individual. When we started the business, I valued tasks above all else. I didn't care who performed the tasks and I didn't care how anyone felt about performing the tasks. I just wanted these tasks done now, done quickly, and done right to move on to the next task. It seemed so simple in my mind, but I could not get my people to do the tasks at the speed, the efficiency, or in the way I needed them done for me (notice I did not say "we") to succeed.

The business was all about me. I had a dream of what my life would look like. The oodles of money I would make, how little I would work. This was MY dream, and I was not reaching it.

Why not?

Because I had no understanding of what my company needed to look and feel like for the people who worked there. I created a business that was all about me, and I left little room or hope for the people working there to see it as anything more than just a paycheck. For that, I was rewarded with a business where nobody cared, nobody was trying hard, quality was poor, and the number of people who were either quitting or being fired was ridiculous. My company sucked and it was all my fault. I needed a "check up from the neck up" as my mentor, Howard Partridge, is fond of saying.

Everything about our company needed to change. I needed to create a company culture where people wanted to come to work. A company where talented people wanted to devote themselves to a higher purpose than just my ambition and ego. I needed to invest in our people and our way of doing business. I needed to attract the right type of team members to our squad and have a company culture that kept them around and excited to work for us. I needed to learn how to create a good culture at work, and quite honestly, I had no idea how to do it.

To fix our broken culture, I looked for training to help me become a better and more aware leader. I saw leadership expert Dr. John Maxwell speak at a conference and I liked his style and his message. So, I enrolled to become a John Maxwell Certified Leadership coach. I was not intending to ever use the information I learned there as my profession, but I wanted to become a better leader for my team and learn how to build the type of company my business partner, Larry, and I wanted to own. For us, we just wanted a company where we actually liked to go to work each day. It was a long time since I felt that way and I know Larry felt the same way as well.

The Maxwell certification was a game-changing experience for me. I learned so much about myself and my weaknesses as a leader. I also learned about my employees, and what they were really looking for in a job. In fact, the week-long training was so intense that at one point, I broke down sobbing because I felt I let everyone down so much. Anyone who knows me, knows that being emotional (other than anger) is not really in my character. It takes a lot to make me break down. In fact, I called Larry that night and told him about what had happened. He could not believe it! He kept repeating on the phone, "They made you cry? Are you sure?" But the training made me see the errors in my ways as a leader and I began to see how many former team members I fired because I thought they were the problem, when in fact, I was the problem. Then I started to realize how many amazing people moved on from our company because we were not providing them an environment where they wanted to work or that they believed in. That realization stung hard and I was very motivated to go home and right the wrongs and fix the company. I made up my mind we were going to create an amazing culture where people felt cared for, safe, and wanted to be in.

Now, let me give you a little warning. If you see this in yourself and get motivated to change your culture by reading this, be prepared for some friction from the team at first. They are not going to believe you.

When I got back to California, I was very gung ho to fix everything. I implemented a daily huddle, much to the chagrin of Larry who viewed this time as a waste of money at first. I started taking my Maxwell lessons and training the concepts to the whole team, thinking this would show them I cared about them and their career paths. I put up dream boards for every team member to post their dreams, goals, and desires. I started asking every team member how they were and if they were ok and happy. I was a man on a mission!

You know what happened? Nothing. They thought I was full of shit.

The team did not believe I cared about their growth or happiness. I never cared before, so why did I all of a sudden give a shit? They also did not like the lessons or the dream boards. In fact, I was making it all worse, not better. I was freaking them out. It all came to a head one day when one of our managers asked to speak to Larry and me privately in my office. He said, "Eric, you have got to stop with all of this personal growth stuff. You are freaking everyone out, including me." I was crestfallen. I went to Florida to get certified (which was not cheap). I was up late each night working on lesson plans to help my people. I felt this was the game changer in my company, and now I was being told by the team's spokesperson to stop. They hated it and they told my manager to speak with me to make it stop. It was not good.

After our meeting with the manager, Larry and I slunk down in our chairs, totally deflated. "What are you going to do now?" Larry asked. My response was that I had no idea. I was at a total loss for words. That night, I went home and took some time to think the whole situation over. They were right, I hadn't cared about them before, so why the change? I was not keen on developing them, so why start now? I realized I needed to slow my roll, keep certain things that I was implementing, and scrap the rest. I also needed, as did Larry, to slowly show that we really cared about them. Until we proved that point over time, all of this was just words. So, I revamped the plan and went back to the drawing board. Here is what I did to gain trust:

I kept the daily huddle. Gone were the big lessons on growth and the dream boards. We started working on small things to make each person's day better in our company. This was our place to start earning their trust and show them that we cared about their day being better. We had an all-team huddle for 15 minutes each day.

I began to hang out in the warehouse most afternoons to help the teams unload their vans and vent to me about their day. It was a small gesture, and often I was just a sounding board for them to tell me about the job frustrations, the difficult client, or just the pain of being stuck in LA traffic.

I began to slowly take an interest in their lives. Not in an invasive way, but by asking them how their night was or what they did on the weekend. I did not make great progress with every team member, but for the most part, the majority were happy that I was taking an interest in them and appreciated it.

I began doing more frequent reviews (monthly) to allow them to understand what we were looking for from them, and letting them know, unequivocally, what winning at work looked like.

DISC training every Wednesday. We used the tool, DISC, to become more involved with how each of us communicated with each other. It was a tool for the team to better understand me and for me to better understand them.

Employee appreciation events. We had a BBQ trailer we used to bring to plumbing supply houses and property management companies for marketing purposes. Now, we started cooking breakfast and dinners for the team to show them we cared.

The above list was certainly not everything we did to improve our culture, but it was the foundation of our new culture. It took time and effort. Creating a good company culture is not something you buy with food or a birthday cake. It is something you build over time by creating a unique work environment where you take care of your people and they in turn take care of the company and its clients. There is no quick fix, but when the culture improves, everything gets so much better.

For our whole team to win, we needed to excel in several areas of our business. Here is a list of the areas we felt were crucial to work on for our success.

THE ROAD TO 7 FIGURES

Building the Person

As I stated above, I lost many potentially great employees over the years through neglect and under-appreciation. As I became a better leader and learned to invest in my people more, I began to come up with a formula to maximize output, buy-in, and retention. I started, slowly, to recognize the need to get to know each person on my team better. To sit down with them, and learn about their aspirations and their dreams. Gone were the public dream boards. Now it was about one-to-one conversations about their future. I was interested in how I could help my people reach their dreams. Too many owners are so wrapped up in their own success journey they forget the people who work for them every day have dreams of their own. We need to help our people reach their dreams, too. Often, owners fear investing in their people because they will "just leave me if I train them too much." That has not been my experience and the great Zig Ziglar has a quote about this concept that I love, Zig stated:

> *"The only thing worse than training employees and losing them is to not train them and keep them."*

So true. How do you grow an amazing business if you are surrounded by untrained team members with no goals and aspirations of their own? You can't. You need to invest in the team, and if you do so, they will invest in you.

People do not leave companies where they are cared for and trained well. People leave companies because they feel nobody cares about them and their needs and desires. If you can tap into this, you will never want for people. Your employee needs will always be met.

Employee Attraction and Retention

Think of the word "attraction" when thinking about getting new employees to join your company. You need to have a beautiful business to attract top-notch talent. Remember when you were a teenager and you started wanting to date? What did you do? You worked on becoming attractive to those you wanted to go out with. Maybe you went to the gym to get in better shape, got the latest cool hairdo, and purchased new clothes. You were investing in yourself to become more attractive to others. Your company is much the same. You need to become an attractive place to work and have a reputation as a great place to work as well.

I visit lots of home services companies across the US and Canada as part of my consulting business. I can generally tell you within just a few seconds of entering the building, in most cases, whether the culture is good or bad in a company. In the companies that are great to work for and are high-performing, there is an energy in the air. An energy of success, of accountability, of professionalism. The buildings are usually neat and tidy. No chaos and no mess. Not fancy, but functional. The warehouse is well organized, the vans are clean, and the equipment is well taken care of. The team members have nice uniforms and are expected to come to work looking good and ready to roll. The employees are happy and talkative. They genuinely like working there. The owner and managers are involved with the team members. They are not sequestered away in their offices, but are available and interested in the team.

Whenever I am at one of these top-notch services businesses, I always ask them about how hard it is for them to find new staff. Nearly always the answer is "not that hard." You see for all those employers who say things like "there is nobody around to do this work," "the young people just don't want to work anymore" and all the other bullshit excuses we all make when we are struggling to find people, we have to ask ourselves one key question: Do I have a business attractive enough to find and hire new employees? Most home service businesses would not pass this test because they have flaws that turn people off. Let's dig into what some of the areas of concern should be for all home service entrepreneurs.

Local Reputation

Most service businesses are local companies. They exist in the communities they service, which is also the same community they draw new employees from. Let me ask you, how is your local reputation as a boss? I mean really, what are your current and past employees saying about you to their friends at the local bar? I can think of several home service businesses I know who have a terrible time attracting new employees but once I visit their shop and ask around, I find out the company has a local reputation as a terrible place to work. It is widely known in town that the owner is difficult, or the business is in chaos, or whatever else plagues these companies. Word gets around. Make sure you create a place to work where people feel valued and they will tell their friends to join them with you.

Online Reviews

What are your online reviews looking like? Does it speak of a company that does the right things and creates happy and satisfied customers? Or are your online reviews littered with complaints and owners arguing back and forth with unhappy clients on Yelp? Do you have a bad reputation on employee sites like Glassdoor.com?

Potential employees will stalk you and your company online to see if you are a good fit for them and their beliefs. A poor online presence will hurt you in finding help.

G.U.T.S.—Secret Weapon

Crucial to our company culture and success was how we viewed our grooming, uniforms, trucks, and shop. These 4 areas were crucial to differentiate our company from the competition. We used the acronym G.U.T.S., as in, it takes G.U.T.S. to be a 5-star service company. We wanted potential clients, and potential employees, to see our team at the gas station looking sharp. We wanted to be able to give a tour of our facility and not be embarrassed about how it looked. None of it had to be fancy or extravagant, just neat and organized. We wanted to show the world we cared about being professional. We wanted to look the part. These little things matter when trying to attract a new hire. People have many options for employment now. We have to earn the right to have them choose us as an employer. Get your shop, trucks, and team looking good to attract people to your team. It may sound like an insignificant thing, but it speaks volumes about your culture and your mindset as a company.

RECAP AND ACTION ITEMS

Most of us business owners initially dismiss the importance of company culture, focusing solely on task completion and profit. After experiencing significant turnover and dissatisfaction within my team, I realized the crucial role that a supportive and cohesive culture played in our company's success. I draw parallels in this chapter to the sports teams from my youth, recognizing that the best teams thrived not on individual talent alone but on teamwork and mutual support. My journey includes a profound personal and professional transformation, guided by leadership training and a shift toward valuing my employees' well-being and development.

ACTION ITEMS:

- **Assess Your Current Culture:** Take an honest look at your company's culture. Observe employee interactions, ask for feedback, and reflect on your own leadership style. Identify areas where the culture may be lacking or where negative patterns persist. Consider how your actions as a leader influence the overall environment.

- **Invest in Leadership Training:** Like the business owner in the story, consider enrolling in leadership training programs. These can offer new perspectives and skills that help you foster a more positive and productive work environment. Leadership development is not just for improving personal skills but also for understanding how to better support and engage your team.

- **Implement Gradual Cultural Changes:** Start small with tangible changes that can gradually enhance your company's culture. This could be regular team meetings to share updates and concerns, creating a more inclusive decision-making process, or setting up informal social events to build team camaraderie. Monitor the impact of these changes and adjust as necessary, ensuring that your actions consistently align with the goal of creating a supportive and thriving workplace.

SEVERAL TRUSTED
MANAGERS SAT ME DOWN
AND EXPLAINED THAT
I WAS NO LONGER IN
CHARGE OF HIRING AND
THAT THEY WERE GOING
TO BUILD A SYSTEM OF
CHECKS AND BALANCES SO
I WOULD STOP HIRING SO
MANY BAD APPLES.

CHAPTER 12:
BUILDING THE RIGHT TEAM REQUIRES A SYSTEM

During the interview process, you are being judged by all prospective hires by how you go about your interview process. So, many home service companies have a potential hire come in, ask them 4–5 questions, and hire them on the spot. No paperwork, no structure, no professionalism, and no sense they had to earn the job. This is not how to go about this. Don't ask me how I know this!

For many years, I did all of the hiring at my company. Alone, just me. I "interviewed" them and I hired them (usually on the spot). You see, I am a seriously impatient person. I usually needed a warm body that could go out in the field and fill a role for me. I always wanted to get the interview process over and done with and move on to the things I wanted to focus on. So, I ran a half-assed interview and as long as they fogged a mirror and were available to start right away, I hired them. No calls to their references, no background check, no input from my team to see if they liked the person or not. As you can imagine, it very rarely went well. I inevitably would hire a very flawed person and then send them off to my team to deal with. It was a recipe for disaster, and I recreated this recipe over and over again. Finally, my team had enough of my antics and performed an intervention. Several trusted managers sat me down and explained that I could no longer be in charge of hiring and that they were building a system of checks and balances so I stopped hiring so many bad apples and started getting real talent in the organization. You would think I would have been offended, but I was relieved. I know I sucked at hiring, I just thought as the boss it was my job, and my job only. I couldn't wait for the new system to be put in place.

To combat my poor hiring style, we created a three-interview-hiring process which only involved me if the applicant made it through the first 2 rounds of interviews.

The 3 rounds of interviews were as follows:

1. The office team, which was all female, would conduct the first interview. We did work in people's homes, so we needed to make sure our female clients felt comfortable having the applicant in their homes. The ladies in the office were very astute when it came to people's character and it was no joke to get past this first interview. The office team called this "The Creeper Test" to weed out people they felt would make them feel uncomfortable in their homes. During this phase, we also had the applicant take a DISC personality profile assessment and a basic math and skills test.

2. The Operations team would perform a fully paid ride along with the interviewee. A manager and a senior technician would take the applicant out for the day in the field to show them what we did and get a feel for whether the applicant was a good fit for the team. At the end of the day, these guys worked side-by-side with this person, so their opinion of the applicant mattered most. My guys also had a very strong "bullshit meter" and knew if the person was a good fit or not.

I was the last line of defense. If the person made it to my office, they had already passed the hardest tests. I just wanted to meet them, since they would be representing our company. Once the three interviews were completed, we had a final meeting to make sure we all still felt an offer should be extended to the applicant and acted according to the group's decision.

I know what you are thinking. How in the world did you have time to do all of this? Well, it was still much less of a time investment to have the interview process than to hire the wrong candidate and have to review, reprimand, and ultimately fire them. This was work, but it helped us get the best talent. It also proved to us that the person wanted the job and was patient in the process of trying to work with us.

In the home service industry, where customer interactions and service quality are paramount, implementing a robust hiring process is very important. I was really missing the mark in those early years and not making it a priority. My team started to create a clear vision of the 5 most important things we needed to do to attract the best talent to our team.

Clear job descriptions ensured that candidates fully understood their roles and expectations. We had to get better about how the company could reach the best pool of candidates, increasing the likelihood of finding future employees who not only possessed the required technical skills but also resonated with the company's values and culture.

Our new structured interview process was vital for assessing candidates consistently and objectively, focusing on both their technical potential and their ability to handle real-life service scenarios. Finally, maintaining a positive candidate experience, regardless of the hiring outcome, strengthens our company's reputation and leads to future opportunities with other talented individuals. Together, these key elements ensured that we could build a team of skilled, motivated, and customer-focused people, who could both create happy clients and not make the rest of the team miserable.

Here are the 5 key elements we changed from my poor hiring style and implemented as we searched for new team members:

Clear Job Descriptions:

- » Well-defined roles and responsibilities
- » Required skills, experience, and qualifications
- » A clear explanation of the company culture and values

Effective Sourcing Strategies:

- » Utilized various channels like our client list, visited local schools, job boards, social media, employee referrals, recruitment agencies, and job fairs.
- » Implemented a year-long, phased bonus structure for team members who brought in new team members who worked out for us.

Structured Interview Process:

- » Consistent interview format and questions for all candidates
- » Use of behavioral (DISC) and situational questions to assess skills and cultural fit
- » Multiple interview rounds with different employees for a comprehensive evaluation

Efficient Evaluation and Decision-Making:

- » Use of scoring systems or evaluation criteria to objectively compare candidates
- » Regular communication among the hiring team to discuss candidates
- » Timely feedback and decision-making to keep candidates engaged

Positive Candidate Experience:

» Clear communication and transparency throughout the process

» Prompt responses to candidates' inquiries and timely updates

» Providing feedback to candidates, whether they are selected or not, to maintain a positive employer brand

Incorporating these elements can significantly improve the effectiveness of your hiring process, ensuring you attract and select the best candidates for your organization. One of the things I did very poorly was not communicating with potential hires during and after the process. I was leaving people hanging and wondering where they were at in the hiring process and, in retrospect, I think my lack of communication was making our company look bad and probably damaging our local reputation as a good place to get a job. Be sure to keep everyone who interviews at your company well informed as to their status during the interview process.

Onboarding

Once you have hired a new employee, you have the opportunity to either "wow" them with your professionalism during the onboarding process, or you can completely drop the ball and just throw them into the job without proper training and have an existing team member "train" them. All too often, we do the latter. I can remember so many jobs over the years where I was thrown in a van on day one with "Frank" the old, crusty technician, and told to "watch him" so I could understand how to do my job. As you can imagine, this is a recipe for disaster. First, Frank does not want me with him, Frank does not like people, especially new people with lots of questions and no skills. Frank is going to treat me like shit and tell me to stay out of his way so as not to slow him down. This type of training happens every single day in the trades, and it really needs to stop. In today's employment market, people do not need to stay at a company that is underperforming in this way. They may stay a day, a week, or a month, but be sure they will leave for greener (and more organized) pastures.

Let's talk about real onboarding—what it should look like and why it's important. We have a few weeks of honeymoon phase with a new hire. They will decide how they feel about the company, how they feel about their future, and decide how hard they will work based on what happens in that crucial first few weeks. That being the case, we need to make sure we are on point with a great training and onboarding system for them to be matriculated into our company.

My good friend, Lisa Lavender, of Restoration Technical Institute, has an amazing program called "WOW-boarding." Lisa joined me and Larry on our Blue Collar Nation podcast to discuss the importance of good onboarding. It is the most listened-to episode in the history of our podcast. Here is Lisa's list of what is required for a good employee onboarding:

- **Exceptional Onboarding Experience**: The program emphasizes making the onboarding experience exceptional to the point that new hires are likely to talk about it positively and possibly influence others to apply. It's not just about giving them a job but making them feel like they are a part of something bigger from the very beginning.

- **Comprehensive Planning and Documentation**: A well-documented plan for the onboarding process is crucial. This ensures that both the new hire and the existing team know what to expect and can engage effectively in the process.

- **Onboarding Committee and Officers**: The program suggests involving the team in the concept of WOW-boarding by establishing an onboarding committee and appointing onboarding officers. These officers are tasked with being consistently positive and engaged in the company's mission, purpose, and values, ensuring a smooth transition for new hires.

- **Employee Retention and Morale**: The WOW-boarding program also addresses employee retention and morale, recognizing the importance of keeping team spirits high, especially in times of labor shortages and increased stress.

- **Capacity and Productivity**: The program acknowledges the need for increasing capacity and improving productivity, especially in light of labor shortages, and offers methods for achieving these goals.

- **Technology and Tools**: Investing in the right technology and tools is highlighted as an important factor for efficiency and productivity in the restoration industry.

- **Cross-Industry Relevance**: While the program is designed primarily for the restoration, cleaning, and construction industries, the principles and techniques discussed are applicable across various trades and sectors, offering universal insights into effective onboarding practices.

Onboarding sounds hard, but it really does not need to be difficult. Just put a few systems in place for the new hire to feel appreciated and to know what they need to do in their job.

THE MISSION STATEMENT

Since we are now hiring all the best people and we have systems and structure to help everyone do their jobs better, we need to make sure we all are heading in the same direction. To do this, we need a concise, meaningful, and often-used mission statement that everyone knows, understands, and can recite at a moment's notice. Do you have an easily understood and memorable mission statement for your company?

Or do you have one of those four-paragraph statements full of jargon that nobody can remember and even you don't really know what it means either? For most companies, it's the latter. Often the owner crafts some esoteric mission statement early on in the company's existence and it gets shoved in a drawer somewhere for time and eternity. I can relate. I did this at first. Then after realizing nobody had any clue what the mission statement said or how it mattered, including myself, I decided to use a mission statement from a friend. It was a good mission statement. It was one sentence that anyone could remember, but it was all about the client. There was nothing else to it. It didn't have a whole lot of meaning to us internally. Then one day, I was out on a bike ride with a very successful business owner friend and while riding, I was complaining about a myriad of problems in my business. He asked me if we had a mission statement, and if so, what was it? I recited our mission statement to him and he was appalled. He said, "Why is your mission 100 percent about the client? What about your team? What about your company? Do they not deserve mention in your mission as well?" I had never thought of it this way, but he was right. Why was it all about the client? What about my people? What about our company culture?

So, I went home that night after my bike ride and began drawing out things on a pad of paper. When I was finally done brainstorming, I created an acronym of our company name (easy to remember) with items to address each area of our business.

Our mission statement became:

S – Service

H – Honesty

A – Accuracy

M – Management

R – REVENUE

O – Opportunity

C – Cleanliness

K – Knowledge

If you notice, there are several elements to this mission statement that I feel are important. First, we used our company name, which is easy for the team to remember and recite. Second, as you can see, there are elements that are directed to the client, such as service and cleanliness. There are elements directed to the company, revenue, accuracy, and management. Last, we made sure there were items for the team as well, especially opportunity and knowledge, as most people desire to advance in their careers. You probably have noted that "revenue" is in all capital letters. We did that on purpose. We wanted every person in our company to understand revenue was the most important thing we needed to be successful. As Zig Ziglar once pointed out, "Money is not everything, but it ranks right up there with oxygen." We helped the team understand we could not have nice things, get people their hours, and grow enough to create real careers and advancement without the revenue to do so.

Frequent Reviewing of Team Members

For many years, I hated to do any type of formal review for my staff. I felt I was always too busy to do them. It seemed like I told everyone what to do all the time anyway, so why slow down for a review? I also didn't like the idea of a review because I was afraid that every time we did one, they would ask me for a raise. However, as we grew, it became very apparent we needed to give formal, constructive feedback on a much more regular basis. It then dawned on me how foolish I had been not to do frequent reviews. How could they get better if they did not know where they stood or what winning in their role with us looked like? So, I created a *Monthly Quick Review System*. It was one sheet of paper, front and back, that rated their performance in key areas. The sheet also gave space for constructive critique, an improvement plan, and the employee's thoughts. I began sitting down with each employee once per month to perform the review. As we grew, my managers were expected to review each member of their team every month. This was one of the best ideas we ever implemented.

I began to notice a trend in my company, that occurred over and over. We would hire a new employee and have high hopes for this person. We would onboard and train the new hire and they would thrive . . . for a while. Then we began to have problems. The further from the hire date they got, often our expectations were not being met. Instead of dealing with the small issues then and there, we would let them fester. We would begin to say, "Suzy seemed so great when we hired her, but I think we got it wrong. She keeps messing up and we may need to let her go." As time went on, our opinion of Suzy would continue to lower, until we parted ways. Then we would start the whole process all over again and find our next Suzy, or Timmy, or Jane and do it all over again. Something had to give. This was exhausting.

I began to look at how we were running our team and I started asking team members why so many of their peers didn't make it with us. The resounding answer was always they did not always know how to win at work. They wanted to do a good job, but they felt like they had to read our minds every day to please us. This was not fair to them. Armed with this knowledge, I began the process of a monthly quick review to explain exactly what we wanted done and how we wanted it done.

At first, each review took more time than I hoped for because we were addressing persistent problems that had gone on for years in many cases. The team was a little fearful at first, but we went out of our way to not make these quick reviews scary or to weaponize them in any way. The spirit of the monthly review was to get on the same page and make sure the employee knew what "winning" looked like in their job and how to make it happen. As time went on, the reviews got shorter and shorter because all of the issues were dealt with so frequently that nothing got out of whack. What ended up happening was if there were issues in a review for a team member who usually got great reviews, we usually found out that they were having problems outside of work and we could rally around them in any way possible.

Here is the review sheet I created to perform reviews very quickly. Should you like the soft copy, just email: eric@supertechu.com, and I will send you the Quick Review Sheet.

ERIC SPRAGUE

PERFORMANCE EVALUATION FORM

Date:_____

Name:_____ Position Title:_____

Department:_____ Immediate Supervisor/Title:_____

Department Head/Title:_____ Review Period: _____ Probationary _____ Annual

INSTRUCTIONS: This form will be completed at the end of an employee's probationary period and quarterly thereafter by the employee's immediate supervisor. The supervisor may also ask the employee to complete a self-appraisal. The supervisor's evaluation is to be reviewed by his/her immediate supervisor. Once the review has been conducted, a copy is given to the employee, a copy retained by the supervisor, and the original sent to Human Resources.

Rate the employee's performance relative to time in position by checking the most appropriate rating. Make an explanatory comment to support your rating, and where possible cite specific examples of behavior that led to the rating. When performance does not meet expectations, list specific goals for improvement and the date you expect them to be achieved.

	Not Applicable	Does not Meet Expectations	Meets Expectations	Exceeds Expectations	Comments
Job Knowledge: The extend to which the incumbent is familiar with policies and procedures applicable to the position and able to work independently.	_____	_____	_____	_____	
Productivity: The volume of acceptable work produced. Ability to organize and prioritize work; utilize time well and fully meet deadlines.	_____	_____	_____	_____	
Quality: The ability to complete work accurately and neatly to meet quality standards.	_____	_____	_____	_____	
Responsibility/Initiative: Acceptance and fulfilment of work assignments, leadership, intelligent decision making.	_____	_____	_____	_____	
Relationships: The ability to establish and maintain effective relationships with others with whom interaction is required in the performance of the position.	_____	_____	_____	_____	
Adaptability/Resourcefulness: The ability to adjust to change with a minimum of disruption to productivity. Ability to contribute useful ideas for improved performance of the position.	_____	_____	_____	_____	

Attendance/Punctuality:

Absences in this review period: _____ days; _____ occurrences.
Latenesses in this review period: _____ occurrences.

	Not Applicable	Does not Meet Expectations	Meets Expectations	Exceeds Expectations	Comments
Supervisory Skills: The ability To get effective results from others.	_____	_____	_____	_____	
Overall Evaluation	_____	_____	_____	_____	

RECAP AND ACTION ITEMS

So many of us don't put enough time and energy into the interview and onboarding process. In this chapter, we discuss the importance of a structured and rigorous interview process for hiring, contrasting it with ineffective methods that lead to poor hires and workplace issues. Initially, the process described involves three rounds of interviews designed to evaluate a candidate's compatibility with the company culture and the specific job demands. We also emphasize the significance of a thorough onboarding process, called "WOW-boarding," to effectively integrate new hires. It highlights the need for a clear, meaningful mission statement and regular performance reviews to ensure alignment with company goals and continuous improvement among staff.

ACTION ITEMS:

- **Implement a Structured Interview Process:** Adopt a multi-stage interview process to thoroughly assess candidates' skills, personality, and fit with company culture. This could include character evaluations, practical tests, and final executive assessments.

- **Enhance Onboarding Procedures:** Develop a comprehensive onboarding program, like Lisa Lavender's "WOW-boarding," to make new hires feel welcomed and valued from the start, ensuring they understand their roles and the company's expectations.

- **Establish Clear Communication and Regular Reviews:** Create a concise, memorable mission statement that reflects both client and team values. Implement a system for regular performance reviews to provide feedback, set expectations, and address any issues promptly, maintaining high morale and productivity.

CHAOS AND DRAMA
ARE NOT CONDUCIVE TO
GROWING A BUSINESS.
WHEN YOU STRUGGLE
WITH DRAMA IT IS TAKING
YOU AWAY FROM THINGS
YOU NEED TO BE DOING
TO GROW.

CHAPTER 13:
TRAINING AND DEVELOPMENT

Your business has lots of systems, they just might not be of your making. Unless you have completely systematized and consistently trained your team on all the tasks in the business, you have every employee creating systems of their own. I am guessing that would not be to your liking. The further the instructions get from the owner's original instructions, the farther off from the desired outcome you usually get. I experienced this in my service business for years. I was not doing the requisite amount of training that was needed to create the user experience that my clients were expecting. This was the cause of a lot of pain and drama in my life and in my business.

Chaos and drama are not conducive to growing a business. When you struggle with drama, it takes you away from the things you need to be doing to grow, and it replaces your time with putting out fires that were created because you did not train your team properly and consistently. This is called "Opportunity Cost" in economics. In simple terms, it means that everything you do to put out fires is a lost opportunity to use that time to grow your business. You are working in a reactive state, which rarely yields growth. This is one of the main reasons small businesses rarely make it to a year in revenue. The owner spends far too much time running around fixing screw-ups and dealing with unhappy clients, and too little time focused on growing a multi-million dollar business where highly trained team members do the work correctly the first time.

TECHNICAL TRAINING:

I am not going to spend a lot of time regarding technical training. I feel there are other types of training that are far more underserved and less spoken about, so we will go into more depth on those trainings. However, every company needs to have staff who are highly trained in the actual service that is provided. This means not putting the newest team member with the more experienced technician and telling him to "just watch and learn." What is needed is to buy or build a system of best practices in your industry to train in. In my industry, the cleaning and disaster restoration industry, we have a governing body (the IICRC) that creates coursework to gain certification and also creates standards (best practices) to do the work the correct way in our industry. We used the IICRC as our base level for training. This way we did not have to invent every training session from scratch. We then used the materials from the IICRC as our in-house training prior to sending our technicians for external training to become certified in each skill within our industry. Having a best practices organization makes training and holding your team members more accountable to doing the work to an industry standard, as opposed to just doing things the way they see fit. Even with all of these resources, it will still be imperative for us to set aside time for group training each and every week. We held whiteboard lessons and also set up practical training in our shop to elevate the skills of our team. We trained together so everyone knew the proper way to perform each task and also allowed us to discuss other potential methods to create our own best practices. This type of training breeds a consistent service experience for the client, fewer mistakes in the field for your team, and time for you to grow the business without having to put out fires all of the time.

SOFT SKILLS TRAINING:

Soft skills training is the most overlooked area of training in nearly all service businesses. In fact, it is so overlooked in the home services space that I felt the need to start a company, Super Tech University, to train home service company employees how to gain strong soft skills.

What are soft skills you ask? Soft skills are the non-technical skills that relate to how you work and interact with others. They are personal attributes that enable someone to interact effectively and harmoniously with other people in the workplace. Unlike hard skills, which are about a person's skill set and ability to perform specific tasks, soft skills are more about the way they do those tasks—their behavior, social interaction, and personal management.

There is an often-quoted Harvard University study that found 85 percent of all business success was due to strong soft skills and only 15 percent was due to technical prowess. That being the case, then would it not make sense to have 85 percent of your training related to soft skills and only 15 percent of your training related to technical work? The reality is quite the opposite, however. Most companies do almost no work on the skills that are so important to the overall success of the company.

Here is a list of soft skills in which the team needs to be trained:

Communication Skills: The ability to convey information to others effectively and efficiently. This includes both verbal and non-verbal communication.

Teamwork and Collaboration: Working effectively with others, regardless of their roles or backgrounds, to achieve a common goal.

Adaptability and Flexibility: Being able to adjust to new conditions and respond effectively to changing environments or tasks.

Problem-Solving and Critical Thinking: The ability to analyze information, identify issues, and resolve problems in a systematic and effective way.

Leadership and Management Skills: The ability to motivate, influence, and guide others. This also includes organizing, planning, and making decisions.

Work Ethic and Dependability: Being reliable, responsible, and committed to one's job with a strong sense of integrity and accountability.

Emotional Intelligence: The ability to understand and manage your own emotions, and to recognize and influence the emotions of others.

Conflict Resolution: The ability to handle disputes and disagreements in a constructive manner.

Creativity and Innovation: Thinking outside the box and coming up with original ideas or solutions.

Time Management: Effectively managing one's time and resources to ensure that work is completed efficiently.

The reason soft skills are so important, especially in the home services sector, is the customer has no idea how to do the work themselves and, therefore, cannot easily judge how well the job was done from a technical perspective. So, they judge what they understand. They judge us by how they felt they were treated. How helpful and articulate the receptionist was on the phone. They judge us by how well our technicians serve them on the job site. They judge us by how well things are explained to them. Grooming and hygiene of our technicians are important to most clients.

The sum of all these small social traits is what leaves people either feeling great about your company or having an experience they would like to soon forget. You see, most people do not complain about poor behavior, they just take their money elsewhere next time and are sure to tell their friends and neighbors how poor their experience with your company was.

To counter my team's lack of soft skills, I began a training program within our company to improve our soft skills. I realized if 85 percent of business success was attributed to soft skills competencies, then this was our competitive advantage in the marketplace. It was highly unlikely my competition was doing anything in this area to train their team. Therefore, I was going to double down on soft skills training to give us a leg up on the competition. We were going to out-serve them and by doing so, get more 5-star reviews online, more client referrals, and more repeat clients. This type of training became our secret sauce for success.

What did the training look like you are probably wondering? Well, at first I had no idea what I was doing. I looked around the internet and tried to find soft skills training for home services, but I could not really find anything. At that point, I realized that I was going to have to just build it myself, so I got to work. I took time each night to build lesson plans of my own and with some trial and error began to figure it out. There was a ton of resistance from my employees at the beginning. They could not understand why we were having lessons about their self-awareness and doing role-playing to better communicate with clients. They bucked me at the beginning, so I had to stay the course and continuously explain why we were doing it and what the benefits were for them. I needed some time to get buy-in. The good news is, as time wore on, they not only began to embrace the soft skills training but also loved the fact that we invested in them. Each day, we taught skills they could use not only at work but in the rest of their lives as well. Although we never intended it, our soft skills training became a great employee retention tool.

We began to see the training paying dividends. Callbacks on our work lowered dramatically. In fact, our industry average for callbacks was 3 percent. Within 6 months of starting my soft skills training, we were at 1.4 percent. We were running at less than ½ the industry average! This was huge for us. Callbacks kill profitability, reputation, client retention, and morale. Even if we would have had no other benefit from our soft skills training beyond this, it would still have been all worth it.

These gains were only the tip of the iceberg for us though. We also saw a dramatic reduction in breakages on the job site, tardiness, and absenteeism, and our 5-star reviews came back up to levels exceeding when Larry and I were on the truck doing the work. It was amazing.

However, the best part of it all was not wasting valuable time having to put out fires all day long. Having to take time each day to mitigate problems and keep clients happy, when the team was not doing all that it could do to make them happy, was killing our business. The opportunity cost of playing firefighter was killing our ability to keep growing. This is such a plateau point for so many business owners and a reason why so few businesses reach seven figures in revenue. You see, the owner spends so much time keeping clients happy, fixing employee mistakes, and generally just trying to keep all the balls in the air, they run out of time to work on growth. This is the great business stalling point. In my client base, it usually happens when the revenue is around $600,000–700,000. The company grows to the point where the owner can no longer be involved in every job and they begin to stall. The owner runs out of time to remain involved in every aspect of the business and then can no longer grow. Training the team on how to make clients happy and having systems in place to make sure jobs go smoothly without owner involvement is crucial to bust past that mark. Soft skills training and training your team to give 5-star service to all of your clients is a crucial element to getting to the next level.

How we began to train these soft skills was definitely a series of trial and error attempts. I would work all day, go home for dinner, then work on lesson plans for each day of the week. The lessons needed to be short (we needed them out the door making money for us), they needed to be easily understood, and they needed to address the fundamental shortcomings my team struggled with. After many attempts, I settled on this formula to create the best possible outcome. It blended our need for them to serve our clients better and also make sure we had elements in the training that would improve our team members' lives both in and out of work. The system was as follows:

Monday: Personal Development

We worked on this because we realized that if our team was struggling outside of work, they would struggle at work as well. Very few people can compartmentalize to the point where if they have personal problems, they won't bleed into the workplace. So, we talked about money management, goal setting, daily habits, and creating the basic skills that create happy and healthy people. Many of our staff liked this day the best as they had never learned this information in school or from their parents, so it added real value to them.

Tuesday: Jobsite Behavior

So many of our problems were caused by our team not having a fundamental understanding of what was acceptable and not acceptable in the homes or businesses of our clients. In these meetings, we discussed minimizing noise, keeping the work site clean and organized, the importance of communication with clients and sharing status updates, and how to make sure the client was happy with how we behave on-site.

Wednesday: DISC Model of Human Behavior

DISC was a game changer for us. DISC is a communication and self-awareness tool that really helped our team members understand themselves, understand our clients, and understand their co-workers. This was the best tool we ever implemented in our business. As we got more involved in the lessons, we began to all speak and communicate using DISC. It was our own special language within the company. In fact, we once had a company from another part of the country visiting us to see our company culture in action. Once the morning meeting was over and the techs all left to work in the field, one of the visitors commented that he felt like we were running a cult. I asked why he said that and he said all of my people were speaking in "some weird language" and it seemed cult-like. What he did not understand was that we worked on DISC for years and my whole team understood that the tool helped us better communicate. They loved how it helped all of us get on the same page.

Thursday: Sales and Service

Thursdays were set aside for sales and service training. We would always do a short general lesson as a team together, then break into smaller groups depending on the individual positions. Our sales techs would do role-playing and strategize to become better at sales. Our non-sales techs would train on the skills to provide 5-star service and client interaction. This was so meaningful to our success. To arm the sales tech with the skills to feel comfortable doing in-home sales in an honest and ethical way was crucial to our growth and to their happiness. For the demolition and restoration team, learning how to better communicate with clients and give a better service experience was a boon to their confidence when dealing with customers.

Friday: Recap of the Week and Quiz

On Fridays, we took the time to go over the content we covered during the week. We would discuss how the team was using the lessons in the field and how we could continue to get better at our communication, our service, and our value to our clients. After a brief discussion, the team would take a 5-question quiz to make sure they were paying attention and absorbing the information.

I cannot express how game-changing this training was for our company. It changed how our team felt about their jobs. It increased their engagement and made them really feel like we were investing in them. We never really set out doing the soft skills and personal development training for that reason. To be totally honest, we just wanted to lower our callback percentages so we could spend more time working on our business as opposed to in it. The benefits we reaped from the training were so much more than we ever anticipated. The team felt cared for, so they cared more. We were investing in them, so they invested in us. Everybody was winning in this equation: the client, the employees, the managers, and us, the owners.

Team Huddle:

Not enough owners will make the time to have the team meet together. They feel if they are paying them, they need to be doing the tasks that make the company money. I will never argue that the team needs to create money for the company. However, I will always argue that the daily huddle will make a company more profitable than companies that do not meet consistently as a team. When I began doing a daily huddle, my business partner, Larry, was dead set against the idea. Larry can be a bit of a bean counter at times and he felt the amount of money we would spend on these daily huddles was cost prohibitive. My argument was we were already spending that much money and much more by being inefficient, having to fix employee problems in the field, lack of technician add-on sales, breakage, and callbacks, and having to constantly train new people because employee engagement was low and we kept losing people. My sense was that, just like the sports teams I played in my youth, getting to "practice" our craft every day together would bring unity, purpose, and skill to the group. Over time, we realized my hunch was correct. We were beginning to build a super team with a super culture by meeting every morning for 15–30 minutes.

So how do you set up a daily huddle and what do you do? Every business is different, but we found this to work the best:

- **Production Meeting (6–8 minutes)**: This is when we went over the jobs for the day and collectively discussed how to win on the job site. Our team had ideas and input on various jobs, so we created a "best practice" for the jobs that day.

- **Soft Skills Training (5–7 minutes)**: As outlined above in the chapter, this is when we poured into our team to help them build the human skills to be winners at work and at home.

- **Van Line Up (10 minutes)**: This is when the management team reviewed van loading checklists, made sure the van was clean and neat, checked that the employee heading out was well groomed and tidy, and made sure the techs had everything they needed for the day, and answered any questions that the technicians may have.

Total Daily Huddle Time: 21–25 minutes

The value of these meetings so far outweighs the expense, it is a no-brainer. We learned this the hard way many years ago. After implementing the daily huddles, our business was doing the best it ever had. We were growing consistently—Larry, the team, and I were all very happy each day.

The amount of drama we had was very small compared to our pre-huddle days. Employee turnover had dropped dramatically.

Everything seemed good for the first time in years. Then we landed three huge commercial jobs within a month. We were ready, willing, and able to do the work on these three monster jobs, but it was going to seriously dwindle our cash flow for months. In our industry, disaster restoration, it is not uncommon to wait months for payment on larger jobs. Therefore, Larry and I needed to float the materials and labor for the three largest jobs in our company's history all at one time. We knew this when we took the jobs, but payment took much longer than we expected. So, as we struggled each week to pay our bills and make payroll, Larry strongly suggested we stop doing the morning huddles because we needed to save money. I could not argue with him on that, we did need to save money, but the daily huddles had done so much to transform our company that stopping them left me uneasy. Due to the stress of our money issues, we suspended the daily meetings and just sent everyone out to work as quickly as possible. Can you imagine what happened? Callbacks and breakages went up, employee engagement plummeted, add-on sales virtually ceased, and everyone seemed miserable.

Why? Because the message we were sending our team was our money was more important to us than them. It was not their problem that we were having money issues. To them, it just seemed that we had given up on them and taken away the part of the job that brought them the most value and joy. We had to do something fast! Larry and I met and both realized we needed to bring back the daily huddle immediately and apologize to the team for taking it away. We brought everyone in the next day, explained how we were wrong to stop the meetings, explained why we did it, asked for forgiveness, and promised them we would never stop the meetings again. You know what happened? Callbacks and breakages went back down, add-on sales went back to normal levels, and everyone seemed happy to work for us again. Eventually, we worked through the cash flow issues and kept on growing. We never could have done that without the team. Investing in our people every day was the key to our success.

RECAP AND ACTION POINTS

This chapter focuses on the crucial role of training and development in achieving business success, emphasizing the need for systematic training to ensure consistency and prevent inefficiencies. We discuss two main types of training: technical and soft skills. While technical training is important, the emphasis is placed on soft skills training due to its significant influence on business success. According to research, soft skills contribute to 85 percent of business success, yet are often overlooked.

Daily team huddles are recommended to foster unity and continuous improvement, proving essential for reducing operational inefficiencies and enhancing employee engagement and retention.

ACTION POINTS:

- **Implement Systematic Training:** Establish a regular, structured training schedule focusing on both technical skills and soft skills. Utilize industry standards and certifications as a foundation for technical training and develop internal resources for ongoing soft skills enhancement.

- **Prioritize Soft Skills Development:** Recognize the significant impact of soft skills on customer satisfaction and business success. Dedicate substantial resources to training employees in areas such as communication, leadership, and emotional intelligence, which are crucial for maintaining high service standards, client retention, and growing profits.

- **Incorporate Regular Team Meetings:** Schedule daily or weekly team huddles to discuss job roles, address challenges, and reinforce training concepts. This practice helps in maintaining team unity, aligning efforts toward common goals, and ensuring everyone is updated and motivated.

KEEPING UNDERPERFORMERS ON THE TEAM CAN LEAD TO DISSATISFACTION AMONG TOP PERFORMERS, POTENTIALLY DRIVING THEM AWAY.

CHAPTER 14:

BUILD THE TEAM OR GIVE UP THE DREAM

My coach, Howard Partridge, to whom this book is dedicated, always preached to me to "build the team or give up the dream." I don't know if that is his saying or someone else's, but I know I took the message to heart. As I mentioned in a previous chapter, I grew up playing on many sports teams as a youth, and the best-performing team always had a strong sense of oneness.

When building a great team, there are several factors that need to be cultivated by the owner to create that winning formula. Here are my top five:

1. **Clear Vision and Goals:** The foundation of a strong team is a clear, shared vision and specific, attainable goals. This is why the Mission Statement is so crucial for your company. Everyone in the company needs to be aligned toward a common objective. Setting clear goals helps in measuring progress and keeps the team motivated. This was crucial for us to become a business.

2. **Open Communication:** Cultivating an environment where open and honest communication is encouraged is essential. What my team loved so much about our daily huddles was it gave them an opportunity to speak their mind and be part of the process.

DISC training also helped us create an environment of improved communication. Having a tool that helped us learn about ourselves individually and then understand our teammates was crucial to building a great team. We made sure our meetings allowed everyone to speak their mind. This included not just top-down communication from me and my managers but also creating a culture of safety to speak openly (as long as it was in a respectful manner) for feedback to flow upward and among peers. Open communication fosters trust, helps in identifying and solving problems early, and supports innovative thinking.

3. **Inclusion:** We all have the need to be liked and be part of something bigger than ourselves. A team brings together varied perspectives, experiences, and skills, which is a key driver of innovation and problem-solving. It was crucial for me to build an environment where everyone could feel like they were a part of something big, something important. More than just a job, but part of a company and a team that was healing society. To do that, we needed to create a culture where we cared for each other, held each other accountable, and made sure everyone felt important. Ensuring that every team member feels valued, included, and able to contribute fully enhances team cohesion and effectiveness.

4. **Professional Development:** We talked about the importance of training earlier. It is my belief that we must train not only as individuals but as a unit as well. Doing hard things together makes us grow closer. It forms a bond that is harder to break. Investing in the growth and development of team members is important. Investing in teamwork is critical. When team members feel that their career aspirations are supported, they are more engaged, loyal, and motivated to contribute to the team's

success. Be sure to invest in your people. If you do, they will invest in your dreams and aspirations, too.

5. **Recognition and Rewards:** Recognizing and rewarding individual and team achievements helps in building a positive team culture. This can be through not only formal recognition programs but also through everyday acknowledgments of hard work and contributions. Appreciation boosts morale and reinforces the behaviors and outcomes that are valued by the organization. In our daily huddles, we would celebrate 5-star reviews, go over the job costing board, and applaud teams that were superefficient on their jobs. We celebrated birthdays, work anniversaries, and new additions to the growing families of our team members. In this modern life, it is easy to go days, weeks, and years with nobody recognizing your contributions. Please make sure your team never feels this way.

We do all of the above-mentioned things in our business to attract new talent and retain the talent we have. In my industry, it costs roughly 1.6 times a field technician's yearly salary to train a new technician if we lose the one we have. That's expensive. However, it is not nearly as costly as losing a project manager for me. A top-performing project manager in my business could be worth millions of dollars in revenue every year. My job is to make sure my PMs are happy, fulfilled, and wanting to stay with me. The road to this is generally impossible to reach by yourself. To grow the business to the size you want, you need to get very good at caring for your team members.

NO BOZO EXPLOSIONS

A while back, I read Walter Issacson's biography of Steve Jobs. While Jobs was obviously a complicated and flawed human being, we cannot discount how he built one of the most valuable companies on the planet at Apple.

Jobs was very clear about the importance of filling your company with high performers. Jobs had strong feelings about having the best talent. He often spoke about the dynamic between A-level employees and underperformers during his tenure at Apple. He emphasized the importance of maintaining a team of high-performing individuals, stating that A-level employees want to work with other A-level employees. They find it demotivating to be surrounded by B-level or C-level colleagues because they don't want to tolerate the lower standards or the extra burden that comes with compensating for underperformers. Jobs believed that keeping underperformers on the team could lead to dissatisfaction among the top performers, potentially driving them away, and thus, he advocated for creating an environment where excellence is the norm, to attract and retain the best talent. This perspective highlights the importance of a meritocratic approach in maintaining an innovative and competitive business environment.

Jobs went on to say, "A players hire A players, but B players hire C players and C players hire D players. It doesn't take long to get to Z players. This trickle-down effect causes bozo explosions in companies."

We don't want to have a "bozo explosion" at our company, but many of us have already had it and we continue to deal with the ramifications of making the wrong hires on a daily basis. It happens to the best of us. The business is growing, we are in dire need to fill a role, and out of desperation, we make a poor hire. The problem is, then we are slow to realize the effect that this poor hire has on our company and how it affects the other employees, your clients, your vendors, and even yourself. Like the frog that gets boiled by the water being slowly heated in a pot, we get used to poor performance until we realize our business is at grave risk by keeping underperformers around. We have all done it. I am certainly very guilty of having done this. I had to learn it was better to let someone like this go and suffer through some short-term understaffing than to keep them around and make all my awesome team players miserable.

Have you ever kept an underperformer/bad attitude around for too long? I bet you have.

Sometimes caring for your people is letting go of the people in your organization who do not fit the mold, don't buy into the culture, or just in general are hard for others to work with or for. Because of this, it is your responsibility to let go of difficult employees and those who are not team players. The surefire way to ruin all the hard work you put into creating an amazing place to work is to tolerate the bad attitudes, the tardiness and absenteeism, the lack of accountability, and the poor work ethic. For the sake of the team, you need to deal with this quickly to save your culture.

LEADERSHIP

None of creating a great culture and awesome place to work is at all possible unless you become a good leader. Leadership. It is such a weird concept. I know so many people who would swear up and down that they are a great leader, yet nothing in how their company runs would suggest they actually are a good leader. Leadership, like soft skills, is a definition that is hard to articulate.

Merriam-Webster's dictionary defines Leadership as:

1. *the office or position of a leader*
   recently assumed the leadership of the company

2. *capacity to lead*

3. *the act or an instance of leading*

What the hell are we supposed to do with that definition? The dictionary can't even pinpoint what leadership is. I feel a better definition is by the world's foremost authority on leadership, Dr. John Maxwell. Maxwell states:

"Leadership is influence, nothing more, nothing less."

I agree with Dr. Maxwell. To be a great leader, we need to gain influence with the members of our team and that influence cannot be positional but relational. What I mean by that is we, as owners, get some degree of influence just because we are the boss—it's positional. The best leader gains influence not by their position, but by the relationships we form with the people who work with us. We need to learn to be that relational leader to be able to grow a business. Take it from me, it's not easy. Many people mistake relational leadership with being everyone's friend, and that will generally not work. Being the "friend boss" can erode your authority and kill your ability to lead. Going the other way by being a hard-assed taskmaster makes people scared and disengaged (don't ask me how I know this!). There is a balance, and it is an art to find out how to do it. It has taken me years to learn how to be a good leader. It has taken me a lot of work and self-reflection to gain the balance of not being too hard or too soft.

My leadership needed so much work that I had to get John Maxwell Certification in Leadership just to run my own company. When I took the certification course, I never thought in a million years I would be a coach or write about it in a book. I was just getting my ass handed to me on a daily basis at work and realized I needed to learn real leadership skills and concepts to be able to take my business to the next level.

I have created a leadership assessment using the principles of John Maxwell's teachings which I use with my coaching clients to get a feel for where they are in their leadership journey. Feel free to take the assessment to see what you need to work on.

LEADERSHIP ASSESSMENT QUIZ

Instructions: For each statement, mark the box that best represents your agreement level, where 1 means "Strongly Disagree" and 5 means "Strongly Agree."

Questions

I actively seek out feedback to improve my leadership skills.

>   1

>   2

>   3

>   4

>   5

I set clear goals and communicate them effectively to my team.

>   1

>   2

>   3

>   4

>   5

I prioritize building trust and credibility among my team members.

>   1

>   2

>   3

>   4

>   5

I am committed to personal and professional growth, and I encourage my team to pursue growth opportunities.

>> 1

>> 2

>> 3

>> 4

>> 5

I recognize and celebrate the achievements of my team members.

>> 1

>> 2

>> 3

>> 4

>> 5

I am willing to make difficult decisions when necessary for the team's success.

>> 1

>> 2

>> 3

>> 4

>> 5

I effectively manage conflicts within the team by promoting open and respectful communication.

>> 1

>> 2

>> 3

>> 4

>> 5

I provide constructive feedback to my team members to help them grow.

- » 1
- » 2
- » 3
- » 4
- » 5

I lead by example, demonstrating the values and work ethic I expect from my team.

- » 1
- » 2
- » 3
- » 4
- » 5

I invest time in mentoring and coaching my team members to develop their leadership potential.

- » 1
- » 2
- » 3
- » 4
- » 5

Scoring System

Total Score: Tally your scores for each question to get a total out of 50.

41–50 Points: Advanced Leader – You embody many of Maxwell's leadership qualities, showing a strong commitment to growth, communication, and integrity. Keep leveraging your strengths and consider mentoring others in their leadership journey.

31–40 Points: Developing Leader – You are on the right path, demonstrating good leadership qualities. Focus on areas where you scored lower to enhance your leadership capabilities.

21–30 Points: Emerging Leader – You have taken the initial steps in your leadership development. Identify specific areas for improvement and seek resources or mentorship to build on your strengths.

10–20 Points: Aspiring Leader – You are at the beginning of your leadership development journey. Consider exploring Maxwell's teachings more deeply and engage in leadership training programs to cultivate your skills.

This quiz is intended for self-reflection and growth. Your score can guide you on where to focus your development efforts.

For many of us, we are a bit humbled after taking this assessment. One of the hardest things to do at work is to lead others. We are all adults, with our own goals, our own strengths and weaknesses, our own motives, and our own likes and dislikes. To be able to guide, cajole, inspire, and move a group of people to the greatness of creating a well-run business is no small feat. You have to learn how to do this to be a business owner.

"But Eric," you may say, "I can't drop everything and just go get John Maxwell certified! What should I do?"

Well, nothing is more valuable than a library card. Leaders are readers! (Or they listen to audiobooks.) The local library has a ton of resources to learn to be a better leader. Here are a few of my favorite leadership books and resources to go find:

BOOKS

1. **How to Win Friends and Influence People** by Dale Carnegie
   This is one of my favorite books of all time. Carnegie's book has sold millions of copies worldwide. It gives us advice on handling people, winning friends, and leading others. Even though the book is decades old, it stands the test of time.

2. **The 7 Habits of Highly Effective People: Powerful Lessons in Personal Change** by Stephen R. Covey
   This book is one of the best-selling business books of all time. It offers a principle-centered approach to solving personal and professional problems. What it really taught me was how to discern what is important from what is urgent and how to manage it.

3. **Who Moved My Cheese?: An A-Mazing Way to Deal with Change in Your Work and in Your Life** by Spencer Johnson
   Of course, I am going to include some John Maxwell books, too.

4. **The 21 Irrefutable Laws of Leadership: Follow Them and People Will Follow You by John Maxwell**
   It outlines Maxwell's principles for effective leadership, each illustrated with historical and contemporary examples. It's considered a foundational text for anyone interested in understanding core leadership principles.

5. **Developing the Leader Within You by John Maxwell**
   This was the first Maxwell book I ever read. I started with this one, as I knew I was the problem. It focuses on personal growth and self-leadership as the basis for leading others effectively. Maxwell discusses the importance of influence, priorities, integrity, creating positive change, and problem-solving among other topics. This book was a game changer for me personally. A motivational business fable, it addresses change management, a crucial aspect of leadership, in a simple and effective way. Nothing ever stays the same, and for some of your team (and maybe you) learning to effectively manage change is crucial to work success and happiness.

PODCASTS

1. **Blue Collar Nation Podcast** by Eric Sprague and Larry Wilberton
   I would be remiss not to mention my own podcast. We have had many amazing leaders on our show from the home services world, such as Tommy Mello, Cheri Perry, Al Levi, Ellen Rohr, Howard Partridge, and Jim McDonough. There are nearly 300 episodes of home service gold in this podcast.

2. **To the Point** by Chris Yano
   Chris has an A-list guest roster of the biggest and brightest minds from the HVAC and Plumbing industries.

3. **HBR IdeaCast** by Harvard Business Review
   The HBR IdeaCast covers a wide range of topics pertinent to leaders at all levels, including strategy, organizational change, negotiation, leadership, and more. It's a great resource for anyone looking to stay on top of the latest in management and leadership thought.

4. **How Leaders Lead** by David Novak
   David Novak, former CEO of Yum! Brands (which includes Pizza Hut, Taco Bell, and KFC), interviews leaders from various sectors to uncover their unique perspectives on leadership, innovation, and success in business. This podcast stands out for its focus on personal leadership stories and practical advice from successful business figures and thought leaders.

RECAP AND ACTION ITEMS

The core message of this chapter revolves around the importance of creating a cohesive team environment to reach significant business milestones, such as becoming a seven-figure enterprise. Several key factors have been highlighted for building a great team including:

- **Clear Vision and Goals**: Establishing a unified vision and specific, measurable objectives is essential. This aligns all team members toward a common goal and facilitates progress tracking and motivation.

- **Open Communication:** Promoting an environment where open and honest communication is encouraged is critical. This includes daily huddles that allow every team member to share their thoughts and concerns, thereby fostering a culture of trust and inclusivity.

- **Inclusion and Professional Development:** Ensuring every team member feels valued and part of a bigger purpose is crucial. The text stresses the importance of professional growth and team bonding activities that enhance unity and personal development.

The narrative also draws lessons from Steve Jobs, highlighting the importance of maintaining high standards and a team of high performers to prevent a decline in company performance and morale, referred to as "bozo explosions."

ACTION ITEMS:

- **Develop and Communicate a Clear Vision:** Regularly reinforce the company's mission and objectives to ensure all team members are aligned and motivated.

- **Foster Open Communication and Inclusion:** Implement regular meetings and feedback mechanisms that encourage open dialogue and ensure all voices are heard.

- **Invest in Your Team's Growth:** Prioritize professional development and team-building activities to enhance skills and strengthen bonds among team members.

YOU'VE GOT THIS! AS LONG AS YOU ARE WILLING TO DO THE WORK, THE ROAD MAP WILL WORK.

IN CONCLUSION:
A PERSONAL LETTER TO YOU TO HELP YOU GET TO 7-FIGURES

First and foremost, I want to make something very clear to you. YOU CAN DO THIS! I know this because if I can pull this off, anyone can pull it off. I am just an average person, of average intelligence, and average skills. However, I have the desire. Desire to be better. Desire to figure it out. Desire to be a success. With that desire is a willingness to work hard. I have missed more than my fair share of time with my kids, birthday parties, recitals, wedding anniversaries, and just being a good father, friend, and husband. I know what it is like to sacrifice to become a success. Like a lot of entrepreneurs, I have failed and failed and failed many times over. I decided to get some help and started piecing together a lot of the concepts that are in this book. I took the lessons I learned and then created my own systems to make it work for me and my style. I tried and tweaked a lot of ideas over the years to create my road map to 7-figures.

Again, and I can't stress this enough, you've got this! As long as you are willing to do the work, the road map will work. It's not always easy or quick, but the concepts in this book are tried and true by many of my coaching clients. My clients Paul and Tina of Spotless Restoration took these concepts and grew from $500,000 to $3.2 million in three years. There was a ton of work and a lot of stress to grow that fast, but they were willing to put in the work and it changed their lives. They are now on a mission to hit $10 million a year, with an end goal much higher than that. Scott Turknett of Pioneer Restoration has grown to $1.5 million very quickly using this system. Scott, like Paul and Tina, is coachable, willing to learn, and works his butt off. Now he is growing his whole team so he can step back from the business and enjoy his wonderful family and spend more time snow-machining in the Alaskan wilderness. Levi Gain is a second-generation carpet cleaner who took over his Dad's owner/operator cleaning business. Levi joined my coaching program a year ago. He didn't quite make seven figures in our first year together, but he will for sure surpass that milestone in a year or two. I have countless stories like Paul and Tina, Scott, and Levi. Regular people doing extraordinary things by working on their business using my teachings.

My point is, the people I just mentioned were no different than you. Yes, they were all smart people who were willing to take a risk and start a business. They were all hard-working. Where they became unusual was that they sought out help to reach their goals and then implemented the plan. That's it. They all just needed a road map to get past that first million.

I am not telling you to join one of my coaching programs. If you do, that's great, I am sure that it will speed up your progress. What I am telling you to do is follow the advice in these pages. Get to work ON your business, instead of always IN it. Put your preconceived notions aside and try the ideas in this book. If you keep doing the same things you have always done, you will continue to get the same results. Follow the people getting those results. These concepts worked for me. It works for my coaching members, and it can work for you. But only if you commit.

So, where to begin? Well, the book started with a long section on running yourself. You cannot build a great business if you are not good at running your life. I tried. It didn't work. So come up with a plan. Take a Saturday and sit down with pen and paper and come up with a workable plan that you can stick to. Make small progressions. Don't overwhelm yourself with so much change that you can't stick with it. Do a few things to get going. A little exercise each day, some time set aside for reflection and thinking. Dare to dream again, and make time in your day to do so. Stop filling yourself with caffeine, alcohol, and crappy food. Start eating better and drinking some water. These little changes will add up over time. As you get settled into your new habits, you will gain the energy and motivation to add more to your self-care routine. Don't let perfection get in the way of "good enough." Just do something to take better care of your mental and physical state.

Once you are feeling better and getting more clear and motivated about how you want to commit to growing your business, start by taking stock of where you are at. Perform a SWOT analysis, and get honest with yourself about the state of your company. Where is it really going, how good is the team, how you are as a leader and manager, and what your financial situation is. Once you get real with yourself about the company and its state of health, you now will have a starting point.

Once you figure out where you need the most work, begin to hatch a plan to fix it. If it's financial literacy, order one of Ellen Rohr's books and read it. Hire a part-time bookkeeper who is familiar with your industry. Commit to reviewing your financials on a weekly basis, no matter how ugly and painful it is. As you do the work, you will begin to make progress.

If it's systems that are an issue for you, find out what is costing you the most money and headaches, and create a plan to build systems to eliminate that problem and get everyone on board to use the new system every day. Once you have tackled one problem, move on to the next most painful issue you have and build a system for that. If you stay consistent and just keep building one system at a time, you will be shocked to find out that maybe only a handful of implemented systems will change your entire operation.

If marketing is your troublesome point, take the advice in Katie's section and just start doing the basics. You do not need to be a marketing guru to get the phone to ring. You can also start to perform referral marketing. Make a few stops a day to potential referral sources. Get involved in the local Chamber of Commerce. All of these small steps add up to big gains, if you just commit to doing it.

Maybe sales is your issue. Develop a sales training program within your company. Set aside a few hours a week to train the team (and maybe yourself) on the basics of selling in an honest and ethical manner. Do some role-playing and create sales scripts that anyone in your organization can follow. These small investments in your time and effort can reap huge rewards when everyone on your team can generate revenue for the company.

Do you lack leadership and managerial skills? Most of us do at some level. Begin to work on it. Listen to audiobooks on leadership while driving, get a leadership coach, read books. There is no shortage of information in the world on the topic of leadership. You just need to be very honest with yourself about how good or bad you really are as a leader and work on it every day. Becoming a good leader who is capable of getting others to buy in to your vision and get excited about doing the work to become a company will be crucial on your journey to reach your goal.

In conclusion, I wrote this book as a reminder to you more than anything else. I wrote it to remind you of the dreams and aspirations you had when you took the entrepreneurial leap. I wrote it to remind you that you are enough and you are totally capable of reaching your goals. I wrote it to remind you to take care of yourself because business is an extreme sport and you need to treat yourself like a business athlete. I wrote it to let you know that no matter how much you may have failed in the past, you are one decision away from success. I wrote this to show you that there are just a few things you need to learn to reach seven figures, and if you can just improve those skills, the sky is the limit for you.

Finally, I wrote this book for myself, because just like you, I struggle with all of the same demons, bad habits, and limiting beliefs we all have. This book serves as a potent reminder to me that I am also enough and I can build as many 7 and 8-figure businesses as I choose, so long as I just follow my own advice.

— THE ROAD TO —
SEVEN FIGURES
YOUR GUIDE TO
HOME SERVICE SUCCESS

7 FIGURE SECRETS

Eric and Katie have helped hundred of companies grow while also building their own seven figure businesses.

Get VIP access to an exclusive 90-minute SUPER training with Eric Sprague and Katie Harris talking about some of their top secrets to success.

www.ingramcontent.com/pod-product-compliance
Lightning Source LLC
Chambersburg PA
CBHW071221290326
41931CB00037B/1774

9 798986 160788